HURRICANE HYMN

& OTHER POEMS

H. R. STONEBACK

ISBN 1-930337-39-6

Some of these poems first appeared in *Aethlon, Florida English, North Dakota Quaterly, Shawangunk Review, Tideline,* and other journals.

Design by Carla Rozman

HURRICANE HYMN

& OTHER POEMS

H. R. STONEBACK

CONTENTS

I *Hurricanes & Tempests: Songs & Hymns*

* *This symbol is used to indicate a space between parts of a poem when such spaces are lost due to pagination.*

II *The Borromean Islands*

III *Variations*

1.

HURRICANES & TEMPESTS: SONGS & HYMNS

HURRICANE HYMN

Hurricane: *a system of rotating wind, originating in the Atlantic or Caribbean, often hundreds of miles in diameter, that travels widely, bringing driving rain and often great destruction* (fr. Carib huracan)

Hymn: *a song of praise or thanksgiving to God, or a song of joy, or ode of praise of gods and heroes.*

How to begin in the wind and the waves?
How do we hymn horrific hurricanes
that blasted the lost coast from New Orleans
to Mississippi, Cameron Parish to Texas,
Ponchartrain to Pass Christian to Biloxi—
where Katrina's gouged a thousand new graves?

Voices:
Blow, winds! Rage! Levee-cracked cataracts—Flee!
The storm-surge flattens the rich rotundity
of Lear-thund'rous coast of ingrate humanity

Hymn (to be sung):
We were sinking . . .Love lifted me, love lifted me
When nothing else could help, love lifted me

Poetry cannot perform search and rescues.
Words are not water or food or shelter.
Grief cannot put a roof over storm-refugees.
Compassion's not a substitute for action.
Come in from the wind, let words restore power.
Come in under the blue tarp of this Muse:

Witness:
Katrina and her sluttish sister Rita
sounds like names of Bourbon Street strippers—
they got a sister, I don't wanna meet her

Hymn (to be sung):
Oh Jesus is a rock in a weary land—
A shelter in the time of storm

Note: since this poem, properly performed, requires the singing of certain lines of old hymns that are useful (perhaps necessary) in the midst of otherwise unanswerable catastrophes, I acknowledge here my debt to the great poets of flood and storm, of higher ground, of search and rescue—the hymnodists of refuge, the writers of old Protestant hymns. In a good old Protestant hymn, the waters are always rising and we are always in need of being saved. In addition, Johnny Cash, Fats Domino, Bob Dylan, and Hank Williams, who are echoed in the "hymn" sequence here, are also in my view important hymnodists. I salute them, too.

Fly iambic helicopters, drop quatrains of wonder.
For the poets storm-stripped of possessions,
hungry, roofless, books lost, manuscripts washed
away, flood-palimpsests, I give five cents a word
for every word I speak here—sound cheap? sound funny?
Let's see *your* mouth-money, raised hands for matching funds.

Memory:
O I know those roads, those rivers, those coasts, those towns,
those bayous, those people, that crawfish country's gumbo-ground
the French Quarter where I lived the sound that cannot be
drowned

Hymn (to be sung):
Rescue the perishing
Care for the dying

Words have consequences (already 193
at a nickel a word). There have been fundraisers
for everybody but poets. The news channels
have had their hurricane moment, time to move on.
Enough tragedy, right? No. Some things must be said.
I see you're worried how long this poem will be—hands please?

Voices:
Among rank rumors of robbery, looting, and rape
a hurricane hymn requires praise not blame, praise
for volunteers who came workers and cops who stayed

Hymn (to be sung):
We are climbing Jacob's Ladder
Every round goes higher, higher

Some things must be heard. (OK, you give a *penny* a word.)
Shall we say, a woman dead in a wheelchair,
hot street, body under sheet, in the sludge-gutter?
Shall we say, a nursing home, all abandoned,
none could walk, all drowned—our mothers maybe?
Rats eating corpses—shall we say all we've heard?

Witness:
"I held tight onto my wife and kids when that flood-surge teared
up the house and smashed everthing and washed her away somewhere
and I ain't seen her since—and they ain't found her body nowheres"

Hymn (to be sung):
Throw out the Life-line! Someone is drifting away
Throw out the Life-line! Someone is sinking today

We hear voices of a vast cloud of witnesses:
One tells of coffins floated out of raised tombs.
Trapped on her second floor, watching gators and snakes swim by;
she hears a banging against the house, looks out,
sees what she thinks is a boat coming for to carry her away,
then sees only a fleet of coffins, resurrected not to blessedness.

Memory:
French Quarter. An old friend in France e-mails to say she cannot sleep
for watching the horror all night. I watch the TV screen
all night with the whole world, looking for places I know, I've been.

Hymn (to be sung):
Yes, we'll gather at the river,
The beautiful, the beautiful river

A poet, fleeing late to higher ground, tells how it looked,
the sounds, the terrible stillness and silence of hurricane eye,
the sudden cessation of birdsong and all motion, and how the horrific
counterclockwise wall of wind rocked down an ancient live oak,
just missing his car. His manuscripts are all gone, his kids are displaced,
and he's consoled by the thought that looters won't steal books.

Voices:
In ruined roofless church open to the sky
voices sing: "While the nearer waters roll,
While the tempest still is high, Hide me, O Hide. . ."

Hymn (to be sung):
Lord, lift me up and let me stand . . .
Lord, plant my feet on higher ground.

Vietnamese fisherman tells how *his* boat roared
ashore, smashed into *his* house a good ways inland,
house and boat obliterated. He praises America,
says he *will* rebuild. All along the coast,
people weep and pick through wave-washed rubble
for keepsakes, holding photos and torn teddy bears.

Witness:
"My mother's house was flattened, but she wants to go,
maybe find one old photo, a Wedgwood plate, one memento"—
(She's of old family there, long in the land, centuries ago)—

Hymn (to be sung):
Leaning, leaning, safe and secure from all alarms
Leaning, leaning, leaning on the everlasting arms

—My student tells me this. Fighting wet eyes, I say: "Hold tight"
and I want to hold tight, her and her mother and that whole coast.
Like Imagist poems, messages flood the TV screen,
crudely spray-painted on shattered sheets of plywood: "Save us!"
"Billy and Flossie OK"; "Have M-16—Looters will be shot."
They sit on front steps, nothing behind them but unbearable brightness.

Memory:
I remember hitchhiking hungry into Biloxi
I remember the kindness of strangers, meals they fed me,
And the gangster who hired me to sing at Trader John's by the sea

Hymn (to be sung):
How high's the water momma?
Well it's eight feet high and rising

I think I see the steps of Beauvoir, the Jefferson Davis house,
with no house left behind them, scrolled images on the screen,
but no commentator confirms the fact. Jeff Davis is forgotten.
I think I remember drinking from a spring in his garden.
And is *that* the blasted house of Father-What's-His-Name, Priest-
Poet-Laureate of the Confederacy? Who said this was about the South?

Voices:
Old man in the rubble says: "Storm's got me reading the Bible, you see?"
Suffering may redeem us, but I cannot forecast the Weather of Theodicy.
I detest atheist prayers in foxholes, distrust all Storm-Theophanies.

Hymn (to be sung):
The night they drove old Dixie down
and all the bells were ringing

I see places on the screen remembered as if in a dream:
grocery stores I knew, served as a traveling salesman,
selling stuff to make signs, advertise their specials—Oh
in those Jitney Jungles and Piggly Wigglies I made signs,

interrogating the text of porkchops and hamhocks,
Semiologist of Cabbage and Turnip Greens.

Witness:
I wasn't eating, saving money to buy tin for my log-cabin roof.
"Honey," cheerful black storekeeper-lady said, "you ain't eating enough."
Later, I found the cooked ham she snuck in my sign-making stuff.

Hymn (to be sung):
  I am a poor wayfaring stranger
  a-traveling through this wearisome land

And those towns, those country stores, are erased from the map.
I want to leave now, lead a convoy of trucks,
carry tons of ham and turnip greens, porkchops
and black-eyed peas and whatever else they want, need,
and make signs, sing songs of enduring and prevailing:
those towns may be gone, but those people will be back.

Memory:
  O City I have loved, more than forty years before the Flood
  O New Orleans, my first Paris, you will rise from muck and mud:
  I cry joy at breaking news: "Fats Domino has been rescued"

Hymn (to be sung):
  Ain't that a shame my tears fell like rain
  Ain't that a shame you're the one to blame

How much more of this can we bear to watch—
Superdome, Convention Center, Interstate;
searchers in boats, spraypainted handwriting
on the walls of Ninth Ward houses, cryptic code,
signs and slashes indicate one dead inside,
corpse to be collected later—oh how much?

Voices:
  Trailing groupie cameras, sleazy celebrities in leaky boats
  impede the rescue, hit all the partisan bickering notes
  the artless heartless snickering politics—every corpse a vote

Hymn (to be sung):
  Come gather round people wherever you roam
  And admit that the waters around you have grown

Mothers wail for missing kids, looters frolic, thugs steal
from the weak and unarmed, snipers shoot at doctors, cops:
but those who take only water and food are not looters
and they shall be blessed in their need as they share

and they shall be damned who steal drugs hospitals need
burn in hell with stolen TVs—Rumors rage, waters rise—Unreal!
Witness:
A preacher says: "Disaster brings out the best or the worst in us all.
Chaos inscribes in blood a hard trail of evidence, irrefutable,
of the human heart's precarious balance of good and evil."

Hymn (to be sung):
And sinners plunged beneath that flood
lose all their guilty stains

But there are heroes, too: neighbors, doctors, nurses;
the black cop who thrust his badge at the camera
and lectured deserters about duty and honor;
the lady cop, blonde hair disheveled—her precinct
in a free-fire zone, where the gangs had more guns
and cars than the cops—sleepless for days, named the curse—

Memory:
I remember the French Quarter cops who arrested me
for singing in the street long ago in another century—Are these
their sons and daughters? Or are they deserters in retreat?

Hymn (to be sung):
and accept it that soon you'll be drenched to the bone
if your time to you is worth saving

—she called the curse betrayal of honor, wept
as she addressed the camera about the need
for a moral and spiritual rebirth
if the city she loved was to be rebuilt—
"But right now," she cried, "we all need compassion."
Saints of the Storm, who never ate, never slept.

Voices:
These and other voices were too real for TV
sound bites shown once and never repeated
too strong: voices hidden, banished from our screens

Hymn (to be sung):
then you better start swimming or you'll sink like a stone
for the times they are a-changing

An officer found this floating in the flooded street,
this message-in-a-wine bottle: "I'm trapped. Please
come immediately with icecold case of Coors Light.
Some shrimp and oysters also appreciated. Thanks.
I'm OK on wine. P.S. I ain't leaving New Orleans."
To be stubborn with style is a Big Easy trait.

Witness:
Solomon sings: Many waters cannot quench
love, neither can the floods drown it. And if love is expendable
(oh how we love our homes) to keep a house, all is condemned

Hymn (to be sung):
I've got a home in glory land that outshines the sun . . .
Do Lord, O Do Lord, O do remember me

Weary of the alternative universe of Cable News,
we turn to the newspapers that pontificate
and the writers who mediate and meditate
the calls for impeachment of incompetent
mayors and governors, rumors of empty trains,
unmoved buses. I turn to the *Times-Picayune*—

Memory:
I remember my old New Orleans paper, how it felt in the hand
as I drank morning coffee at the Café du Monde,
how they noted my protest songs, trolley-tunes, civil rights demands

Hymn (to be sung):
How many seas must a white dove sail
Before she can sleep in the sand
The answer my friend is blowing in the wind

—but if you read all night the online *Times-Picayune*
and all their reader e-mails with details on every street
and neighborhood you enter a separate singular world

where the blame may still be general (local, state and federal),
but nothing sounds like it does in national news.
It's best to listen, while you read, to Fats, or jazz funeral tunes.

Voices:
"There is no way to imagine America without New Orleans.
This great city will rise again." "Do it right. Listen
to these words: Integrity. Accountability. We are Americans."

Hymn (to be sung):
The water is wide I cannot see
nor have I bright wings to fly, build me a raft . . .

At least you will avoid the frumpy dowdy prose
of *New York Times* writers who refer to our Cathedral
as a "Disneyland Castle Backdrop," spout clichés about blues,
Dixieland, chichi restaurant-talk, Mardi Gras and all that.
And you will learn that chaos and dysfunction are universal,
but all truth is local, and all grief, and we are all born to lose.

Witness:
"We got no use down here for them anal-lectual bureycrats
wanting to measure us for relief, measure this, measure that.
Ain't nobody but God kin measure where my lost wife and kids is at."

Hymn (to be sung):
Born to lose, it seems so hard to bear
When I awake and find that you're not there

I keep dreaming of kids in a schoolyard
remembering a waking dream from long ago
voices of children laughing and chanting game-rhymes
outside the window of some place where I stayed
somewhere on that coast or in New Orleans—
Saint Ignatius I think the school was called.

Memory:
I don't know where that schoolyard was, but its trace
through memory rings clear and it leads from the waste-
land of my youth to the Saint's exercise of Composition of Place

Hymn (to be sung):
I'm a pilgrim and a stranger wandering thro' this world of sin
On my way to that fair city, when the Saints go marching in

That first time, hitching and walking in on old US 90 from the Pass,
through Waveland (now gone), I got to the Quarter late,
climbed the fence in Pirates' Alley behind the Cathedral,
slept in Saint Anthony's Garden. It was a trick of sanctuary
I'd learned on the road: sleep in or against the wall of a church.
In the early morning a priest woke me, the sound of early Mass—

Voices:
Harden not your hearts. The sea is his, and he made it—his hands
prepared for you a place on the unquiet earth, on the high land.
Build your spirit's home beyond the vast presumption of the human.

Hymn (to be sung):
When we gather on that high ground, and the gates are closed within
I'll be shouting "Glory, Glory," when the Saints go marching in

—echoing from within. Priest brought me coffee and beignets in the garden
and warned me about the cops. Later I learned that Faulkner used
to live across the alley. Soon my name was in lights on Bourbon Street—
with luck and a thirty dollar guitar, through the kindness of strangers,
priests and gangsters, strippers, bouncers and bartenders, Garden District
millionaires, Tulane girls, gentle old jazzmen, folksong fans who pardoned—

Witness:
"Don't be messing with that tall skinny white kid—he's family,"
the old jazzman told them all. "Don't come around here asking for union fees,"
the gangster told them, "no musician union in my club—Stoney works for me."

Hymn (to be sung):
When the Saints go marching in, when the Saints go marching in
O Lord I want to be in that number, when the Saints go marching in

—(or collected) my eccentricities. Preservation Hall was open, but I preferred now-defunct Dixieland Hall because Walter played God's trombone there, with Cornbread Thomas on clarinet. I used to walk Walter home, carry his trombone—he had a bad limp—across Rampart into "back-a-town" near the old St. Louis cemetery. Some said it was a bad place. Nobody ever bothered me. I ate in Walter's kitchen. I had never heard—

Memory:
And oh the jazz funerals and "Just a Closer Walk with Thee,"
echoed down the years in "Last Walks" in the islands, Eleuthera, Bimini,
Guadeloupe, but no band ever played grace or moved like New Orleans

Hymn (to be sung):
Just a closer walk with thee,
Grant it Jesus is my plea

—the trombone played that way. Once Walter came to hear me sing at my club. You know how it was then—he had to come in the back door and stand in the hallway. It hurt Walter to stand, so I asked my boss if he could sit, right down next to the stage. A good guy, he said yes.

Hell of a good guy for a gangster, he always said I was under his protection. Wanted me to get out, go to college. Now Walter's house, and everything—

Voices:
"Fair Play for Cuba" Lee Harvey Oswald chanted in the street
outside my apartment. In the Absinthe House, Garrison talked conspiracy.
The Sixties had started. Nothing would ever be the same again—Oh freedom.

Hymn (to be sung):
Will the circle be unbroken, bye and bye Lord bye and bye
There's a better home a-waiting, in the sky Lord in the sky

—is under water, and they are all gone and I love, I bless them all.
And that schoolyard is gone, that school is gone, and those kids
are gone somewhere but I still hear their voices like an ancient song
that echoes above the miraculous roofs of the flooded world.
O come back again mysterious horns and gentle souls to those blessed
streets where, the rankest sinner, I first heard the Voice of God call.

Witness:
I will make a pact with you Katrina and you too Rita.
It was you who smashed the old wood and new, obliterating
beloved country and city. I curse you, your brothers and sisters.

Hymn (to be sung):
And I'll stand on the ocean until I start sinking
And I'll know my song well before I start singing
. . . It's a hard rain's a–gonna fall

Or consider this pact: if I praise your hurricane curves,
the elegant wrists of your winds, eloquent breasts of your waves, sleek
ankles of your rising, haunting stillness of your eyes, your divine destiny
decreed by weather-gods in Noah and his wife Joan's Book of the Ark,
will you kindly take your striptease, your dirty little dance,
somewhere else, some deserted coast, some lonesome sea-surge.

Memory:
Who was it who said: "This storm proves God is like So not Dead."
Was that the same TV program where the commentator said:
"It's time to move on. The country's hurricane moment is over, ended."

Hymn (to be sung):
Like a bird from prison bars has flown
I'll fly away

Dear America, the Country of Tomorrow, always fleeing the Past,
even if it's only a month ago, and a half-million are still lost, displaced.
And no one wants to talk about *Rita* and Cameron Parish, where all
is bedraggled and derelict, where the last tree left standing holds
diluvian decorations—shredded banners of bedsheets and clothes
like dry leaves before the wild hurricane flown and all through the House—

Voices:
"We must relearn humility and compassion and it does not matter
where or how we learn it, in the storm, or in the gutter,
and we must live it and not talk about it, kill it with chatter"

Hymn (to be sung):
Rock of Ages, cleft for me
Let me hide myself in thee

—not a creature is stirring because there *are no* houses
and there will be no Christmas in the Empire of Forgetting.
But I see there's a relief auction of Britney Spears' underwear
and soiled flip-flops on e-bay so maybe everything will be OK.
Besides, we live in a country where 200 million pounds
of ice can be moved around the country for weeks in a crisis—

Witness:
The truck driver said: "I picked up 20 tons of ice in PA, hauled it
to Missouri, then to Alabama, then up to Virginia for a week, stalled
there, truck run for a week to keep the ice frozen, waiting for a call."

Hymn (to be sung):
Why can't I free your doubtful mind
and melt your cold, cold heart

—well they called him, sent his load of ice to Nebraska; he unloaded
it into government-rented storage freezer. Not one ice cube melted.
"Dragged that ice around," he says, "two weeks, 4,000 miles, never used."
Truly wondrous country, where 4,000 truck drivers can drag 90,000 tons
of ice all over the map for two weeks and not one ice cube gets lost.
Enough to make you want to mix a real tall gin and tonic and get loaded.

Memory:
When I was twelve I sold Italian Ice from a red barrel I pulled
around on a red wagon. So much depends on ice. Later I hauled
stuff all over in a big rig for Allied. In the Marines, I liked beer ice cold.

Hymn (to be sung):
Jingle bells, jingle bells, jingle all the way. . .
Never send to know for whom the bell tolls

Robert Frost worried whether the world would end in fire or ice.
He favored fire, but if the world perished twice, ice would suffice.
When Rita struck, I saw on TV a motel on lowground by the Gulf,
surrounded by fast-rising waters. A few years ago, I stayed there.

They were very nice people. I forgot an old tweed jacket, left it
in the room. Had the usual important things in pockets—pen-knife,

Voices:

When I told her I'd just done some poetry readings in San Antonio
was on my way to read in New Orleans she said "Oh I wish I could go
I love poetry but I've never been anywhere but here minding the store"

Hymn (to be sung):

The water's deep and the water's wide, Hallelujah
Milk and honey on the other side, Hallelujah

coins, scraps of notes for poems. I didn't miss it until New Orleans. I called and talked to the sweet Mexican girl who ran the store attached to the motel. We had talked about poetry and the world the night before. I meant to give her one of my books, but I forgot that too. She said she'd mail my coat right away. When it arrived, neatly packed, all contents intact, I read the note she'd written:

Witness:

"I really enjoyed talking to you about poetry. Nobody talks much
about poetry around here. I was embarrassed to tell you I write some
too and I wanted to send a poem with this but I haven't got the guts."

Hymn (to be sung):

The water's deep and chilly and cold, Hallelujah
Chills the body but not the soul, Hallelujah

I wrote back to thank her, and with my check for the postage, I sent her a copy of my book of poems about springs and water and floods. She wrote back, said she loved my poems, was memorizing some of them. Said she was writing a poem about how it's scary living on the Gulf edge. Said she hoped to get to college before she was thirty, but she couldn't leave her folks alone to run the place. Said if it got good enough she'd send—

Memory:

I remember how I felt age ten when I met my first real published poet
and he gave me a copy of his book I thought it was really neat
and it might be cool to write, even go to college, so much world to see

Hymn (to be sung):
Michael row the boat ashore, Hallelujah
Michael row the boat ashore, Hallelujah

—me her poem about water. I never got it. I was away for a long time.
That was years ago, and I'd forgotten it all until I was sure I saw that
motel and store, that girl on TV last week, fighting, sandbags holding back
Rita's rising sea. I've lost the phone number, the address, the name
of that motel on a back road in the middle of nowhere. I can only pray
she is not one of those washed away, missing forever, in the briny—

Voices:
"Hey! Over here!" He got his family out, stayed behind to go
to church, got caught. Trapped in the attic 16 days, 76 years old,
no food, a gallon of water. Now he's found, saved—only wants a Taco.

Hymn (to be sung);
Let the lower lights be burning!
Send a gleam across the wave

—Abyss of the Gulf. All knowledge is local, all grief, all love.
Bless me Father I have sinned. Bless me Katrina, Rita, I hate wind.
In the name of the city, the country, and the holy Spirit of Place.
(If I could find her I'd send this poem now, ask her to send her poems.)
Listen, did you hear that? Forty years ago, I heard it as they did two
hundred years ago. Above the brooding waters, the raven and the dove—

Witness:
—It is the ghostly voice of Père Dagobert chanting in Jackson Square
the Kyrie Eleison: relief workers heard it last week the oldest prayer
the people's litany: In an ancient city nothing is simple except prayer

Hymn (to be sung):
Kyrie Eleison: Lord have mercy upon us
Christe Eleison: Christ have mercy upon us

Do we really understand? Do we get it yet? Can we comprehend?
Hiroshima, they say, flattened three square miles;
9/11 was confined to a few blocks; now extend that
400 miles, from Manhattan to Montreal and beyond; or, think

from New York to North Carolina—thousands of square miles—
devastated. Where does rebuilding begin, and how will it end?

Memory:
the voices of children singing in the schoolyard: toxic ditches
I sat upon the banks of Ponchartrain at sunrise in the 60s, fishing
I remember even atheists singing old hymns in the kitchen

Hymn (to be sung):
Some poor fainting, struggling seaman
You may rescue, you may save

So let us hymn the heroes: Cops, Firemen, Army, Navy, Air Force, Marines, Coast Guard, National Guard and all the volunteers; that Bourbon Street Bar that never closed; that search and rescue team that lifted 4,000 people from rooftops in two days, the PJs sliding down cables bringing MREs; ground-pounders doing knock-and-mark neighborhood sweeps, zipping body-bags; neighbors who cared, survivors who shared, nuns and priests:

Voices:
The Katrina-Rita Diaspora, scattered in fifty states helter-skelter,
a half-million homes destroyed; they huddle in motels and shelters,
they try to dream a song of rebuilding, remaking lives lost in the welter

Hymn (to be sung):
Amazing Grace, how sweet the sound
that saved a wretch like me

And as the graygreen mold rises, voices say: "Build an endless mall of dreams,
a highwalled nature-free zone with themed Jazz Villages, Old South Villages,
Cajun Villages, one vast casino-coast—Bourbon Street a hundred miles long, where it'll always be Mardi Gras never Ash Wednesday."
(In Russia, they want to dump Lenin's fungus-sprouting syphilis-ridden corpse—"horrible mummy"—
Some leftover 60s Lefty says: "Install it in the Peoples Republic of New Orleans.")

Witness:
"Good for Tourism," he says. "The future of this whole coast is Disneyland."
The People said: "We've got news for Con-men & Comrades in Katrina-land
—this is our *place,* our *song; we'll make it new with* our *vision,* our *hands."*

Hymn (to be sung):
I once was lost, but now am found
Was blind, but now I see

After all the hurricane hymns and penitential psalms we will go back again
to the last real city in the authentic country of the giants who flourished
before the flood, and they will come back with joy and horns and songs,
and we will walk The Street again. And all along that ravaged coast we'll
dance
at Cajun Fêtes, Bless Shrimp Fleets, eat Michelin-manna, pray at
Cathedrals
and *be* in that miracle-number when Sinners and Saints go marching in.

Memory:
I'll have a Dixie beer at the Napoleon House, maybe eat at Galatoire's
even Antoine's (old neighbors); feed a hungry poet at the Maple Leaf Bar
(she'll be new in town from some motel on some lost coast); maybe I'll hear
Fats Domino, or Walter's grandson on trombone, voices in the schoolyard

ATHEIST SINGS HYMNS IN MY KITCHEN

For Donald Junkins

Eternity happened in my kitchen,
one of my graduate students said,
written in the face, the voice, of the poet
from Amherst—tremolo-trembling, chin lifted,
eyebrows steeply arched, head bobbing up
and down like one of those bobblehead
figures, tears streaming down his cheeks
as we sing hymns for hours, long after midnight,
singing "In the Garden, " "Lord We are Able,"
"I Love to Tell the Story," and all the rest.

(While I play guitar and sing I wonder
if the best poets are all lapsed Methodists.
He studied for that ministry until he fell
into the writing classes of Robert Lowell.
Did he ever sing hymns like this with Plath
and Sexton, with Lowell and Roethke?)

In between hymns someone whispers: "It's the start
of a new school of poetry—the Hymnagistes."

(Thinking well maybe it's just lapsed Methodists—
who always were the best singers and songwriters—
I crank the guitar into a new hymn,
thinking of Pound and music, melopoeia,
phanopoeia, and logopoeia, and how

this is all three simultaneously.
At least it is for me.
Of course, I've done my time with Methodist
sermons and hymn-sings. I wonder if somewhere
a nonlapsed Methodist preacher is at this
very moment chanting our poems with a trembling visage,
late, after Sunday certitudes and grape juice,
intensity inscribed in the lines of his face.)

The hymns pour, a timeless placeless hymn-sing.
Like old nights longer than flesh, the hymns linger.

(I think of old friends in China, even Party officials,
who belted out hymns they'd learned from missionaries
in the days before hymnbooks were banned.)

The Professor from Texas, a poet
and a Catholic Pilgrim, lights his pipe, dances.

The Poet from Boston, a Unitarian,
and a professor, doesn't know our hymns.
Perhaps a case of terminal Bostonitis?

I watch my old friend's face, paint it on guitar strings,
try to recall the first time we sang hymns—
on some island boat-dock? or on a careening bus
going too fast down a treacherous mountain pass
in Austria? The Hymnagiste altarcall winds down.
Poets go out into the altered night, heading home.

Around 3 AM he says when the singing's over:
"I might be a lousy atheist but I won't let those creeps
take Jesus away from me, no sirree, they can't take Jesus
from me!" No one thought to ask who the creeps
were who would take Jesus from him—we all
just seemed to know. When he repeats his atheist
line more colorfully, his old compadre,
the deep-voiced Professor from Delaware,
ostensibly asleep in his chair rumbles:
"You're not an atheist, you're an agnostic."

I wish Chinua Achebe had not gone home early.
His father was a missionary—I bet he knows old hymns.
A good guy. We compared notes on wheelchairs,
someone called us Wheelchair Brothers.
Even if they all thought he was wrong
about Heart of Darkness, he must know some songs.
Maybe Conrad was the creep who took Jesus away.
But that's not a very Polish thing to do.
Maybe it was Kurtz? Either way, it really hurts,
especially when atheists from Massachusetts
weep hymns in your kitchen at 3 AM.

DWELLING IN BEULAH LAND: HYMNAGISTE SONG FOR CATHA

"Thou shalt no more be termed Forsaken; neither shall thy land
any more be termed Desolate . . .thy land Beulah: for the Lord delighteth
in thee, and thy land shall be married" Isaiah 62:4

Once, you told me over high noon champagne
under steep cloudless mistral-cleansed Camargue
skies, how, just a girl in America,
you sang the old hymn about dwelling in
Beulah Land, where no one is forsaken,
the land is not desolate, and the people
are married to the earth in the Lord's delight.
Beulah, Bunyan's Land of Peace, where pilgrims
progress, drink from fountains that never run dry
and all things are in bountiful supply.

Was it in Hollywood you sang that hymn?
With Margaret O'Brien? Did Richard sing
along? Or was it on that New Place island
off Florida? (And where did I sing that hymn,
a hungry child wild in the vast chaotic
coast-to-coast camp-meeting of America's
raucous revival in the wilderness?)
And where is Beulah Land now, what progress

have we made, Pilgrim, and how do we dwell?
It's such a swell word, *dwell*, all dwarf-dwindled
and solitary in the dictionary.
Old Ezra came to me in a dream-station

of the Philadelphia subway, chanted
softly "Beulah Land," said he'd learned it in
Sunday School in Jenkintown or Wyncote
(at that church near that fake Wanamaker
Castle where my grandfather socialized),
said he was trying to find his way back,
there or Idaho, could I show him the way.
Said his sleep was troubled by the thought of what
America would be like if the grand
old hymns still had a wide circulation.
We sank, hummed the hymn, "in contemplation,"
though still he shunned the thrice-rhymed "salvation."

Old hymns are starting to come back to me—
did they ever leave?—their musical sequence
now clean, free from emotional slither,
no more fear of metro(g)nomic weather
and time, or rhyme: Let's go, Catha, and dance
in the garden, hymn Beulah-words from the sea.

SONG FOR ROSA PARKS

(On her last ride: Detroit, 25 October 2005)

In 1955 I was too poor to ride a bus
and when I had a nickel for school busfare
I saved it, walked four miles to junior high.
I knew even then I'd give you my seat
if I had one, give you the bus if I could.

A poor white kid living in a northern slum,
I watched the world and I wasn't so dumb
I didn't see what you did and how it changed things.
And I remember how it made me sing.
And how it made me feel about walking.

Our school had bad troubles and race-rumbles
but still we played ball, made music together.
When I went to the homes of my black friends
it didn't matter that their houses were nicer,
they wore better clothes, their parents had cars,

TVs, and telephones we didn't have.
They never made me feel ashamed of being poor.
(Like suburban kids at summer camp did).
My best friend in '55 was Vincent Cream.
His father was Jersey Joe Walcott, heavyweight champion

of the world. (You'd change your name too wouldn't you?)
Vince lived on the good side of town, across the tracks.
At his house he had a TV and we watched Rosa Parks,

pictures from far away in Montgomery,
the beginning of a new song on TV.

And I'll never forget the words of Jersey Joe Walcott.
Looking at the screen, the champ said: "Lady's got guts."
Repeat after me: the champ said twice—*she's got guts.*
I don't remember much else from way back then.
I moved south, lived hard and fast, it all passed

sooner than a song. I lived in Alabama,
I liked almost everybody there, white and black.
Even those who warned me not to sing certain songs.
I sang in places from Anniston to Dothan,
Sang Hank in Montgomery, sang Gospel, sang Freedom Songs.

*

For a spell, I was a traveling salesman,
making signs and selling felt-tip pens and magic
ink to country stores and supermarkets—
Piggly Wigglies and Jitney Jungles
and nameless country crossroads shacks—

and all those people were kind and good to me.
Then I worked in the woods outside Wedowee—
some locals thought I was a little crazy:
a kid from nowhere building a log-cabin the old way,
skinning pinelogs, notching everything into place,

talking about writing the Great American Novel
while his wife worked long hours at the City Café.
All song, all the best poetry, is testimony,
witness: So this is just to say, Rosa Parks,
at least one poorwhite kid in a northern slum

was moved and changed by what you'd done, and how
you did it. (Like the headlines say, quiet courage
and dignity trump anger, outlast rage.)
You moved north, I moved south, and Alabama

moved with us. When I left for New Orleans

(then Hawaii, Nashville, Paris, China, New York)
Alabama went with me. You did too.
I remember, just before I left,
how the deputy sheriff (that my friend from up north
called a thinlipped redneck racist) told me:

"Alabama would be a better place
if we had more Rosa Parkses. Yessir,
it's people like her what make this a great state.
Some day coming. And don't quit singing
them songs you was born to sing, kid."

I knew then Alabama would be all right.
I knew things would be worse in Camden and Detroit.
That was 1962. The long walk of memory
always yearns toward a boycott of the past.
I had almost forgotten, the way I forgot

what I wrote and left behind in the log-cabin
I never saw again. Later, I heard
some locals saw my handwritten poems
on the mantel over the fireplace
in a rundown house up the red-dirt road

from my cabin—"ol' Jim's place," they said,
"that *kellered* feller worked at the sawmill,
his wife a-setting there, stitching that quilt
in that rocking chair, saying them poems"—
or maybe I only dreamed that, Miz Rosa,

  like some old song we sang on a bus ride
  like some old freedom-dream you gave a kid

REMEMBERING APRIL 1968 OVER MORNING COFFEE IN ANOTHER CENTURY

(Janitor— Keeper of the door who sees both ways—from Janus)

On April 4, 2006 I write these words,
remembering an old April that I hold
in ways I had almost forgotten:
Thirty-eight years ago today they shot
Martin Luther King in Memphis. I studied late
and alone on the deserted Vanderbilt
campus—like most graduate students
I heard no news. Didn't hear the muted
sound of riots in the streets. Didn't know
he'd been shot. Then the old janitor rolled
his trashcart into my silent TA den
in the dim basement of Old Central.

—(Do I have to say that Vanderbilt's in
Nashville, in the South, and they shot Mr. King
down the road, and Old Central's where Agrarians
pondered *I'll Take My Stand* and segregation,
and the janitor was a black man of great
dignity, a friend who taught me much about
the trees and plants and other things that grew on campus)—

He told me. Wordless silence wound around us.
We listened to excited voices on
his scratchy portable radio. Dawn

was a long way off: sirens, tanks came closer.
We said nothing. Then he almost whispered:
"Things always gets bad before they get better.
Pray Jesus we all get better together."
We shook hands. He put his hand on my shoulder
the way a wise old man knows how to do,
said: "Get home safe, be careful where you go."
I climbed into midnight stillness, West End
Avenue eerie and empty, only the wind:

Took my usual route through Centennial Park,
then saw all the troops and trucks, kept walking
until they seized me by the concrete Parthenon.
Held two hours by National Guard in Athens
of the South. Many tanks, soldiers in jeeps:
I was in forbidden terrain, in deep,
a space-and-curfew violator. They checked
me out, walkie-talkies crackling, finally let
me go home to my place in the blacked-out street.

Not much else happened that April. I passed
my PhD Orals. Bobby came to town,
then they shot another Kennedy down.
Then there was Gene, that season of my last
campaign—I'm still glad I sang for McCarthy,
the right one, though some said the wrong party.
(Years later, when I saw Gene give a keynote
at Princeton, on Fitzgerald, his literate wit
confirmed my old choice.) In China, Cultural
Revolution raged. In France, radicals
shut down the country. In Prague, the tanks came.
Later, leaders and victims of all those games
would become my friends, in all those places
and more, bound by *Soixante-Huit's* horror and grace.

But what I remember most, and hold tight today
is the way old Moses the *janitor* prayed
we'd all get better together: and his hand
on my shoulder, his voice, the Promised Land
shining beyond fire and flood to the *Keeper*

of the Door, the voice that keeps repeating:
Things get real bad before they get better.
We're strong at the broken places together.

DELTA DAWN . . . ZELDA'S GONE

Delta Dawn, what's that flower you have on?
Could it be a faded rose from days gone by?
And did I hear you say he was a-meeting you here today
To take you to his mansion in the sky?
(Song: Alex Harvey & Larry Collins)

Was it at Vanderbilt or on Music Row
that I first heard the story of Zelda,
after Scott was gone, on a visit home
to Montgomery from the Asheville sanitarium:
In a long black dress, face shrouded by black veil,
standing on a street corner handing out religious tracts—
Repent now! Atone! Save your soul from Hell!
The story was told by a supposed eye witness.
Maybe somebody in Montgomery really knows
if the Queen of the Twenties, the flaming jazzrose
consumed by the fires of desire and despair,
really did these deeds and preached these needs in her
intolerable dress of flaming rose turned black
and if from her tragic vortex she ever looked back
and if she was redeemed from fire by fire.

Oh Zelda, Save me the Last Waltz and pray
for me now and at the hour of our dance
and how can we retract our wasted youth
and how shall we redact inexorable truth

In the late '60s I told my Nashville neighbor,
a songwriter friend, to quit bugging me

in my yard for song ideas while I studied
for my PhD Orals. "Go read some Faulkner,
some Fitzgerald," I said. "Steal from them."
So he did, and came back with "Delta Dawn,"
number one hit in the world before long.
The song is part Faulkner, part Fitzgerald,
part fire and ice, in sterling cup, well stirred.

Oh Delta Dawn did you know that Zelda's gone
and how she left us when the fire died down?

Oh Zelda Dawn what's that flower you've got on?
I cannot see your hawk's eyes behind that black
veil, so I cannot tell as you walk the streets
and hand out tracts, if you're looking for Scott,
hoping somehow to save him, save yourself,
hoping he'll take you to his mansion in the sky

"GOD'S TROUT: FISHER KING & DELTA FORCE RECON THE UPPER TIGRIS"

At the secret source of the most ancient river
where the very Tree of Life shadowed Eden:
there, on the upper Tigris, the mysterious trout—
alabalik—lurks among unfished rapids
and riffles where Kurds contend with Turks.
Mines bloom on the banks of Baghdad-bound waters.

Far downstream, Iraqi troops fire thousands
of rounds into the river. They say a pilot
has descended from the sky, hides in the river:
a fanatic crowd cheers as they shoot the water,
set the riverbank reeds on fire—in deep midstream,
trout hold steady, then ascend toward Eden.

Upstream at midnight Delta Force regroups beneath
the appointed bridge: twelve men (who do not exist,
it is said) gather in susurrous darkness,
greet one another with handsigns and whispers,
exchange the secrets of reconnaissance,
then wait, more certain than the wide water's silence.

Another man joins them sometime towards dawn:
tall, bearded, in local dress—austere, humorous,
he says he has been fishing with grubs and worms.
He says there is a rare trout in these waters—

alabalik—it could be translated "God's Trout."
He once caught one, he says, in the Garden.

Since he works for the CIA, he does not explain
his more cryptic remarks, though he does note
that "God's Trout" defies mere science, should not exist here,
by evolutionary laws. "Go ask Noah,"
he says and then they freeze at the motion
downstream; through nightvision goggles they see the glow

of a boy fishing: they watch him catch big trout
and release them with some gesture of blessing.
At first light, the boy climbs the bank with one large fish
and vanishes to the south. Overhead, a missile
soars towards Kirkuk. Then they hear singing—alert
under the bridge, they watch dozens of men, women, children

walking barefoot on the rivertrail, barefoot and singing,
walking north. When the Force comes up from the river,
standing and stretching in the warm sun, they do not look
like CIA, Special Ops, Delta Force: they look local,
and hungry. Heading south to the next village they have
ascertained to be secure, they relax, tell jokes,

talk about fishing, how war is good for trout—"take
certain Croatian streams," one says, "unfished for years
due to riverside mines—the trout are yours for the tickling."
The CIA man says he wants to fish for the red-speckled
alabalik, he must get back to the Garden.
The smoke of cooking-fires rises from the village

as they approach, salute those who know them,
sit down by the river where food is brought to them.
The trout, charred over hot ashes, taste like God's Trout,
they say, laughing. The village elder explains
that the people who just passed to the north
are Assyrian Christians on yearly pilgrimage

to the Garden of Eden, to drink the source

of the Tigris. "The others moving along the river
are fleeing the Siege of Baghdad." He makes a sign
with his hand and more perfectly-cooked trout are brought.
Many people from the village are eating
by the morning river where no one is fishing.

The village chief and elders exchange intelligence
with their visitors as they eat. Planes pass far
overhead. "You will need luck in Kirkuk,"
the elder says, putting something in the leader's
pocket. At the fire, the Force sees the boy who came up
from the river with one fish. He is cooking many

trout, many men with the boy, many fish cooking.
The Force moves down the river. Now they say nothing.
Men who own the night do not name who owns the sky.

PULP POETRY—50 MPG

The editor-in-chief, the big boss
of a legendary literary press,
sits in my library, after lunch, tells
me over wine about all the books pulped
every year, sold to ethanol producers—
when I hear the facts, I'm shocked, I gulp
my wine, look nervously at my books—
she explains how the efficiency experts
fix the proper ratio of stock on hand
to sales and warehouse waste. (I'm consoled
by the thought*: 'Tis better to have been published*
and pulped than never to have been published at all).
She names famous names, their rank in pulpdom,
and I feel a secret delight in this wisdom
and think of the way of all flesh and how
'tis better than never to have been pulped at all.
Late, after she leaves, I am deeply pleased
with the secret knowledge that my poems
might power cars and tractors and backhoes.

I've got a secret: I know who's being pulped.
I won't name their names—that would be betrayal—
better to let professors and their students
retain their innocence of pulped icons
and other shocking matters like the fact
that a leading university press
demanded a five-figure "subvention"
from the editor of the best *Collected Poems*

of one of our greatest poets. Let classrooms
keep their naïve and non-commercial dreams.

That night I go to sleep thinking about *pulp*—
"a soft moist mass of matter, shapeless"—
thinking that's what most poetry is, yes,
either that or *pulpit* poems. Even in sleep
I edit my etymology: *pulpa*
has a different root than *pulpitum*
(still we seek the homiletic lectern
to affirm that flesh can sustain spirit)

I dream the answer to who was most lonesome:
Descartes or Pascal or Hank Williams.
Then I wonder if records can be pulped--
can we turn songs and poems into pasta?
I see Ferlinghetti as my dreams move faster,
and I laugh at the off-rhyme with spaghetti
and think he's right that most poetry now
is prose all dressed up in typography:
food, fuel, e-motion—*he should know (let it be).*

Yet the dream lingers that books live forever,
endlessly resold at Library Sales and Goodwills,
used bookshops and Salvation Army thrift stores,
passed down lovingly from hand to hand,
ascend to heaven of Abebooks or the Strand.
But at last I know what the old term Pulp Fiction
means: I hold the mystic key to all ignition.

Exact even in dreams, I ask how can it pay
to ship tons of books from New York to Georgia
to be pulped? I dream of buying a truckload,
of hijacking a big rig full of unsold poets
on the Jersey Turnpike, giving away books
at every gas station all the way down I-95
to Georgia. In my dream I drive a curious hybrid
sports car streamlined like a sonnet. The model logo
reads *Corvette Petrarchan.* When the dream-scene shifts
I'm driving an understated pickup truck

with a model-blazon *Imagiste* or *Hymnagiste*—
I can't be sure due to mud-splotches. So much depends
upon a muddy pickup. (Stick it in your gas-tank, pal).
Then I drive a John Seer tractor, the *Dirt Libre* model.

I fill up at pulp stations with pumps marked
Random House Regular—40 MPG guaranteed.
Simon & Schuster Super claims 45.
New Directions Poet-Octane advertises 50.
So I fill up on high-quatrain fuel,
and, all the hijacked books given away,
drive home to finish my next book of poems,
serene and blessed in the knowledge of sure
and certain pulpdom, knowing that my lines
will someday fill the tanks of strangers driving
to nightclubs and churches, weddings and funerals,
knowing at last that poetry does make things happen,
reading the interstate signs like a faux-Baedeker,
singing and sitting on my arse poetica,
sure that the true Art of Poetry
is "To Teach and Ignite"—
a poem should not mean, but drive.

ON THE ROAD WITH MOM

For Jack Kerouac

Maybe that's the thing about all these beatniks
the reason why in my teenaged Fifties
on my own folksong troubadour-raging road
I could quote them but I never really felt connected
with them—it wasn't their drug culture
and their homophilia that made them alien,
that made me, even though I knew *Howl*
and *On the Road* the minute they were out,
identify more with Woody & Hank & Fats
than with that coterie of Jack and his cool cats—

Jack, living, traveling everywhere with his mother,
in his 30s, 40s even: unthinkable—
long bus rides from Orlando to California
with his mother, living with her in Florida in that tacky
house in bland subdivision neighborhood where he wrote
The Dharma Bums in his naugahyde recliner chair
parked by the air conditioner.
Don't get me wrong: I love my mother, of course,
even if I didn't see her or talk to her much
between the ages of 12 and 30.
I assure you, just before writing this poem,
as a kind of meditative Composition of Place, I called her
and not long ago, for her 90th birthday,
I wrote her a poem. (She liked it very much).
But still, I never wanted to live with her
since I was 5 or maybe 7, and I'm quite certain

she never wanted to live with me.
Is it some Protestant-Virgin-Mary-Deficiency
in my bones that compelled me to run from home
as soon as I could and never go back
unlike old Catholic Jack the Kerouac
who on all the raging roads never left home
until, seeking some dharma-momma vision of heaven,
he drank himself to death at age 47?

AND SHE LIVED A LONG DEATH

She died a long, long life
and she lived a long death
telling us all, for years,
that she would not be here
very long, she'd be gone
when we got back from where-
ever, and we never
knew what to say to her—
nonsense you'll live forever?—
we all knew things were bad
and she might not live through
the day, but she told us
so for years and years: (I
vowed I'd never do that;
who knew the occasion
would present itself soon?)
I'm in a far country
and the phonecall comes late—
(after the fall of fate)—
the connection unclear
in Havana: "She's gone."
I did not know what words
to say. But she has left
me with this code—although
I have felt my death for
five years worth of midnights
I won't say it in day-

light, I won't make you un-
comfortable, speechless.
(So please forgive me if
I didn't say *Farewell*—
it's such a lovely lone-
ly word I want to mean
it if I get to say
it not dull it and kill
it with repetition).
After all, it's our long
dying together, al-
ways, that makes our living
lovely and possible—

FOR ONE OF MY CHINESE STUDENTS

When I lived in China in 1984 I learned many things
from my students. One day when I was sitting
in the gilded pavilion by Lake No-Name giving
guitar lessons to Chinese students (they stood in line
and waited patiently for ten minutes of instruction)
this sweet kid who loved Hemingway learned his chords
quickly then told me that he heard some other students
saying I was not like other "cheese-smelling foreign devils."
He said that was what they called most Westerners.
Before that Spring was over he learned to eat cheese
and drink wine with me. We got the imported brie
and camembert and wine at the Friendship Store
or from friends in the diplomatic corps.

He liked cheese and wine almost as much as he liked
Hemingway. I helped him with his rhythmic tight
translations of Hemingway's "Up in Michigan"
and "Today is Friday." He was warned
not to publish them, but he did anyway
and he was censored, interrogated—almost jailed—
by the Communist Party puritan thugs who dictated cultural
matters. I told him he was "pretty good in there today."
He smiled, said nothing. He made Hemingway sound right
in Chinese. Later, he wrote a long poem dedicated to me
and gave me an elegant scroll he'd made
with the powerfully delicate strokes of his calligraphy.

I was there with him in Beijing in June 1984.
We laughed, then, because it was as he said "Orwell's Year,"
and everything was going well, freedom in the air.
I was not there with him in Beijing in June 1989
when he carried the Goddess of Democracy into
Tiananmen Square.
I was not there when he was shot and crushed by the tanks.
His family does not know where he is buried.
I do not know where he is buried.
I do not know what to do with this poem for him.

STONEY KISSED A CATHOLIC

The first girl I kissed was named Joanie Riley—
fire-red hair, Irish, the only Catholic in our
Protestant neighborhood: The adults said
we were the cutest couple, laughing as they took
pictures of us holding hands: I was six, she was five.

Later, fifth grade, another Protestant slum.
I wandered into the Catholic ghetto
just a few blocks away and kissed Doris West.
Word spread like wildfire—by the time I got back
to my block where mostly Methodists lived
the kids on the corner and the front steps
all chanted: "Stoney kissed a Catholic—
Stoney kissed a Catholic." Well, I confess,
I *did*: next day her six older brothers beat the hell
out of me—fists, sticks, tire chains, blood everywhere
but I fought back hard. Then of course we were friends.
I liked her brothers better than I liked Doris.
Once I bought them all grape popesicles.
Later we all played on the same football team.

For a while, I thought I knew the secret of Original Sin,
echoed in the chant: "Stoney kissed a Catholic."
And I was a proud Methodist mystic—
sure of my vocation to teach the girls this:
Methodist rhymes with kissed.
I *had* my methods and they almost always worked.
But there were times like that day with Kitty,

the prettiest girl in the school—I walked her home,
deep into the far country of the Italians.
But that's another story, a bad one, switchblades, zip guns.

Somebody here is thinking Oh what a sorry,
narrow, violent world religion makes—but you've missed
the point. I *miss* that world of neighborhood codes
where people knew who they were. From the security
of boundaries you could negotiate identities
and achieve what adults called *lasting peace.*
And besides, that's where we got our mystics,
from chants like "Stoney kissed a Catholic."

FULL FRONTAL POETRY

For JK & my other stripper-neighbors: Bourbon Street 1963

She said:
  "Are you pleased by full frontal poetry
  or teased by tasseled sonnets in lingerie,
  by forms holding tight Victorian secrets,
  shaped stanzaic mysteries, uplift discreet?"

He said:
  "Do you like poems free and Triple X
  or mystical, blazing with sin and sex,
  God and grace—spinning in burlesque discipline,
  economy of surrender, chaste beginnings."

FORTUNE'S WHEEL: OR, THE GAMEKEEPER IN THE WHEELCHAIR

Funny how you'd never noticed before—
the form, shape, design, the stuff of wheelchairs.
Like this World War One vintage rig pictured
in an ad for a BBC miniseries,
Lord Chatterley in curved highback wooden
chariot, his Lady behind him, one cool
solicitous hand resting on his shoulder,
the way that women do when men are struck

down by fortune's wheel, men who used to look
down from on high at varicolored roots
of parted hair, and lean low to push long locks aside
to kiss the back of her neck. Now, seated thus,
viewing her world at eye-to-breast level,
no more need for downhill stolen glances,
a new, direct perspective on cleavage,
on lips and eyes looked up to—all's topsy-turvage!
And that cool elegant hand on the shoulder
laying claim, or saying down boy, down:
The hand of all the nurses dreamed by soldiers.

Suddenly at sixty, the humble gamekeeper
hunted down, laid low to the ground, grim reaper's
earthy joke: "See the world another way,
everything made new, see Naples and die."

In a wheelchair you watch too much TV,
you hear voices talk about "wheelchair sex,"
about some professor somewhere in the west
who shows videos of wheelchair sex therapy
in his seminar on human sexuality.
"Why should taxpayers pay for this," intones
the voice from deep within the no-spin zone.

(Why do people at college poetry readings or places
like the *Knitting Factory* cheer when you say "breast"
or "sex?" "Do it with brakes on? off?" "See Naples and die ..."
Wheelspeed down the volcano—"See nip- . . ." and—
What is this—the Super Bowl halftime show?
It's all a matter of perspective and position,
looking up looking down, longing and location
And Oh that cerulean harbor, chthonic Vesuvian breasts)

Oh let cool slim hands spin the scandalous wheel
of obscene fortune; let shell-shocked warriors
sink into their chairs, transfer into cars
in bonewracking pain, and spin and shift
and tough-talk to nurse: "Check this out. Watch this"—
then make some fancy move that rattles ribs.
Alone, late at night, surf the web, seek the beach-
wheelchair that rides the sand, rolls you in the surf,
where breakers crash and mermaids sing and waves
lave lava-locked joints that cannot run from Pompeii:
get your blasted bones back, at last, into the sea.

ON THE MYTHICAL MYSTICAL DOMESTICITY OF A HYPHENATED POET TURNING 30 (AS IF IT'S 60)

OK, so we all succumb, at last, to the mastery
of time, aging, death, loss, bleak pain and grief
but do we have to talk about it, must we write
about it? why not wage war against it with song,
with words and deeds. Enough of 30-year-old poets
accepting their limits, their smallness in the scheme
of things. Here's a few words—*screw age, screw loss*—
that will cost you nothing more than 60 years
and the complete breakdown of your flesh and bones.
There are better things to do with words than mourn.

The hyphenated poet with a face like an omelet
and quirky quizzical eyes like umlauts
(and legs like commas—you notice things like this
more from wheelchairs), as she turns thirty in self-pity,
wants me to mourn the auspicious cost
or her domestic circumscription—her loss
of magic, of enchantment, to sing austerity
with her in gorgeous syllables—here's a kiss,
blow out this candle darling, make a wish:
There are better things to do with age than mourn.

THE ASCETIC POET'S SONG OF PRODIGAL AUSTERITY & AUSTERE PROFLIGACY

of course we want what really is
what only the imagination gives:

the plainest sense of things
where still the spirit sings

the extravagant facts of dailiness
the particular acts of frailties

reclaiming some small glory before death
some radical love of all we have left

LE RETOUR DE LA FÉE VERTE

The Green Fairy has returned! Absinthe
is legal again in France: Hyacinth-
girls dance in *les nuits blanches* of Baudelaire,
sleepless nights in the yellow fog of care-
lessness. Banned during the Great War so men
could stand to fight (and myriads die in mustard winds),
the faithless fairy freed from alembics
floods the green earth dressed in jazzy iambics
dreaming of *vers libre*—inebriated
poets drip-drop lines and lives created
like baleful exercises in writing classes:
Symbolisme, DaDa, Beat, Hip-Hop, Surreal Masses!

HUNTING BUNTING: BASIL VARIATIONS WHILE READING *BRIGGFLATTS*

For Basil Bunting: 1900-1985

stone-smooth skin
mason's mallet chiseled in
original sin
we all serve a life sentence,
excrement and innocence
love's a convenience
like indoor plumbing
death's easier than remembering,
dying's as easy as forgetting
self-rapt, self-hating, begetting
sluttish solipsist squalor
cheap tricks three-for-a-dollar

Basil: sweetest herb, royal
intoxicating aroma, with afterscent—
in the garden—somehow deathly
ceremonial like a basilica.
Why do they have the same root?
Bunting: all the flags, the festive cloth,
the cone-billed birds, the infant's snuggery,
Pete Rose butt-bunting to first base—
First Basil, then all the rest of the royal
aromas of the gods' good garden dirt.

Who knows his name, who cares? I scan his book
in one hand, type this with the other,
looking through wine for lines to bend and twist.
His editor thinks "I am agog with foam" the best.
I detest it, and weary with this exercise,
I sing "Bye, Baby Bunting," eschew paraphrase.

Most great poetry has the taste of gothic garlic
the romanesque scent of basil
rhythmic rhymes like wine and shapes like olives
and edges like the infinity belvedere
above Amalfi, sea-sheer Ravello.
With strong songs sung a cappella—
shun the key of B-Flat and who needs the goat-star—
voices in the chapel: we know where
we have been though all the maps are lost
and we do not need to guess
where we are going

HUDSON HAIKU: JANUARY MORNING ON SOUTHBOUND COMMUTER TRAIN

I
Ice slips south, the sea
Knocks it north: raw rhetoric
of estuaries

II
Winter robs the river's
Glibness, August-palimpsest
Simplicities

III
Winter clouds remember
Nothing: in the snow every
Thing comes closer

IV
Bannerman's Island:
War detritus snores in Seven
AM moonlight

V
Storm King: gunrunning
Sun rakes cliffs of Nada—
Hail! St. John of the Ice

2001-2008

HUDSON RIVER LIGHT

I
Did you ever notice how when the train
glides along the Hudson River at Six
AM on a winter morning, under
a full moon, with fresh-fallen snow coating
the river ice not yet disturbed by passing
barges and tugboats—how the frozen
time-stopped river looks so narrow and houses
on the cliff of the West Shore look so near,
just a snowball's throw away? Does the snow
and pale-moon-ice make all things come closer?
That is how it is in the bone-zero
beauty of this morning's motion, southbound
Hudson train, January 11, 2001.

II
And now the sudden subtle purple dawn,
the morning mauve flows west from the Taconics,
pink trying to be purple rides across
the river ice: *I have never seen this before.*
It lasts less time than it takes to write these lines.
Light-waves wash up West Shore cliffs, toward pale moon
and then, abrupt as they came, they are gone.

Rapt, I think of the twenty years I lived
utterly inside the light of this river.

III
The old rough-stone cabin known as The Roost
perched on that rock that rises from the water:
Twenty summers, spring and fall, we watched
a thousand sunrises, sunset, moonrise:
Twenty years of song wound in the wheel
of the day, the night, the slow seasons.
We measured the hours by the bells of Holy
Cross, the monastery next door. We waited
for old John Burroughs to walk some midnight,
seeking silver drops from the sturgeon's leap.
His old place two doors down, where his family
still lived at ruined Riverby. Moonlight keeps
all its secrets by ancient rivers.

*

Every morning at sunrise, coffee on
the shingle beach. Then the dive, first swim
of the day, a little fishing, a quick sail,
running with the wind. It was impossible
to write inside that light with the river
flowing through your bones and your bonfires.
I had a floating chair, foam cupholders;
I planned to float all the way to New York,
to the sea—once I made it to Poughkeepsie,
drifting, until the tide turned me back.
I had a notebook but waves washed my words away.

Now the river still runs through my bones
and maybe that's why I have a dry land floating
chair: It's my river, my light, I own it.

IV
The last time I *stood* to give a poetry
reading I felt my bones collapse before
it was over. That was *Café Millennium.*
The last time I stood to teach was 9/11.
The sky that month (when I first rode a wheelchair)

was clearer than the mysterious springs
of Florida I'd been diving too deep, too deep.

V

When I lit up the bone-scan like a Christmas tree—
I laughed: *"That's the Hudson flowing through me."*
The river has come closer, very close.
The river brings all things down, down to size.
It's only the light that rises and survives.

BALLAD: THE CROW'S RANSOM NOTES (*DERRIE DERRI-DA-DOWNE*)

For Jacques Derrida: R.I.P October 8, 2004 & For D.A.

I was preparing a concert performance
of "The Three Ravens" when the invitation
came to do a keynote on John Crowe Ransom
and the legacy of the New Criticism

with a downe derrie derrie derrie downe downe

They wanted me to speak of how Ransom
had been held hostage by literary theory
in recent decades, his views distorted,
the New Critics vilified by disciples

with a downe derrie derrie derrie downe downe

of Derrida *they said*: my mind was inside
the old ballad, which version to sing, about
the crows or ravens which pluck out the eyes
of the beloved gentleman, or the satire

with a downe derrie derrie derrie downe downe

But the heart of the ballad is the death
of the new slain knight and how the faithful mourn:
his hawks, his hounds, the fallow doe, and how

the crow's dark ransom is redeemed by love

with a downe derrie derrie derrie downe downe

The nonsense refrain echoed behind my eyes
all day until I read the *New York Times*
and learned of the death of Jacques Derrida
from a dim ill-tempered obituary

with a downe derrie derrie derri-da downe

The song still sang in my head as I read
of Derrida's so-called *defense of Nazi*
De Man and how *Deconstruction* led only
to *Nihilism* and the *Death of the Canon*

with a downe derrie derrie derri-da downe

Then it came to me how I'd heard all this
before, when they tried to bury the so-called
New Critics who were my teachers at
Vanderbilt—I knew how they read what they loved

with a downe derrie derrie derrie-da downe

And when I lived in Paris I had learned
a different Derrida—the man who said
I love the Canon! who sensed all the ghosts
who read, like Ransom, the vanished author

with a downe derrie derrie derrie-da downe

Both men turned into *false schools* by puritan
dogmatists who plucked out their eyes their vision:
narrow *americademics* who could not
comprehend the work of mourning, the death

with a down derrie derrie-ransom-da downe

of the author, the scripture of otherness,

and how uncertainty is always at
the heart of belief. Both men betrayed by false
disciples—*plucked out their eyes and ate their*

with a crow derrie-ransom-da downe

barthes the crows the crows the ravenous foucaults.
They die so *primly propped so sternly stopped*
(as John Crowe Ransom sang in his old ballad)
and all I want to do now is sing for them:

with a downe derrie derrie derrie downe downe

No keynote no crowing just this song to mourn
and take my place among the faithful few
as ghosts pass: *God send every gentleman*
such hawks, such hounds, and such a leman

with a downe derrie derrie derrie downe downe

FAREWELL, FAREWELL UNTIL WE SING AGAIN

For The Posse

Farewell, farewell until we sing again
Let us hold these hymns together my old friends
And as we rise into the light
and we sink into the earth
and we fall like crystal waters over stone
We sing to the rising sun all our ancient sacred tunes
Till we find a home beyond these ravaged bones

Litany (modal chant):
  Every day begins another pilgrimage
  As we write our lives in love not rage
  As we catch the fish that must be caught
  and teach the ones who will be taught
  and sing the songs that must be sung
  and sing the world into silence and love

Farewell, farewell until we sing again
Let us hold these hymns together my old friends

Litany:
  On golden mornings a posse of pilgrims
  Follows timeless roads across France and Spain
  Key West to Kentucky Gravel Switch to Flatwoods
  country-fried communion and all the songs are good
  and we detest the sins but love the sinners
  and when we reach the end we'll know the beginning

Farewell, Farewell until we sing again
Let us hold these hymns together my old friends

Litany:
We write our lines to leave our sons and daughters
We drink from sacred springs of holy waters
And refine old orders of holiness
And define new visions of blessedness
And when we begin to feel posthumous
And the world holds us as God's hostages
We sing from prison cells pull down thy vanity
And we all sing Hallelujah Anyway

(Repeat complete first stanza)

Farewell, Farewell until we sing again
Let us hold these hymns together my old friends

Is this a poem or a song or both? After more than four decades of working as a poet and a singer-songwriter, I am frequently asked to speak about the intersections, the crossroads of poetry and song. I sometimes say: "A poem should not mean but sing." And I am never entirely satisfied with that formulation. In any case, this song may also be a poem; perhaps it reads as well as it sings. As a song, it is included in the CD Album: Live at the Oasis: Stoney & Sparrow—Songs of Place 1962-2006.

2.

THE BORROMEAN ISLANDS

I. *ISOLA DEI PESCATORI*

We must travel far until we come
to an island with no bridge, no cars;
it must be an island with a café
and no cars; let it have one small elegant
hotel with a fine waterfront restaurant;
let there be a ferry to transport us
to the mainland, if we must go across;
let us cherish the hour the ferry service
ends, the tourists all gone, the island ours
again; let this island with no cars be
a place where cats sun themselves on the docks,
strut unalarmed in the middle of what
passes for a street, and human footfall
in cobblestone lanes dictates the rhythms
of island life, as we stop in the middle
of any lane and salute the day's order
of things with cats and neighbors that we meet.

Let it be an island with no cars,
a café (where Frederic Henry and Hemingway
stopped), a well-run hotel clean and cheerful,
with all *les plaisirs de la table*
in the restaurant in the garden
on the terrace by the lake where we eat
four local fish courses caught by our
Fishermen's Island neighbors in the morning
sun, where even lake-loud comminatory Alps
do not disrupt what the cats have to tell us
about fish and fishermen, about ourselves.

The hotel referred to in this poem is the legendary Hotel Verbano on Fishermen's Island in Lago Maggiore, off Stresa, Italy. It was the lakeside hideaway of Toscanini (and other famous people). A portrait of the Maestro hangs in the lobby next to a framed copy of this poem.

ISOLA BELLA

Among these islands they have owned and shaped
for eight centuries, in their lake, they come and go,
the Counts and Cardinals of the clan Borromeo—
even a Saint in the family, San Carlo,
though I cannot imagine him staying
here in this Palace, which he would not approve:
He walked this island in its natural form,
before this Palace, before these Gardens.
Down the lake at Arona his vast statue
oversees and blesses the Borromean waters.

I know that Manzoni, Flaubert, Stendhal
and all the rest praised this baroque island—
did they even go next door to Fishermen's
Island? Manzoni probably did. Was it
mentioned in their Baedekers?—but I cannot
praise this domain, this most famous island,
the goal of every tourist. The Palace
makes me edgy somehow, maybe it's the thought
that Napoleon and Mussolini slept here.
My mind wanders as a guide describes the Stresa
Conference, Benito and Laval and McDonald
in this Music Room among the Flemish
paintings—was that before or after Hitler
called Mussolini "My Teacher" and Benito
called Adolf "The Buffoon"? Ah well, if things
don't work the way you plan, if you can't keep
Hitler out of Austria, you can always invade
Ethiopia. (Then, too, there's the fact

that the liberating armies are moving north,
and there'll always be a mob around
to hang your battered body upside down.)

Here, in the Great Hall, Princes of Church and State
have long gathered under the Borromeo
Family Motto inscribed on the dome:
Humilitas.
That's it, yes, we build, we make, we create,
then we crown our works with mouthed humility.
Maybe this, too, makes me nervous, edgy.

We go down in the cool grottoes, the lake-
level basement, made for natural AC
almost 400 years ago, where late
Lunatic Baroque designs run amok:
Underwater scenes, stone mosaics,
and shells, shells everywhere, arching over
bizarre collections displayed in cases.
It is cool here—but it's not the kind
of place to have a cold one, relax, catch
the Yankees playing the Red Sox on radio.
I touch sharp shells, commune with mottoes, grottoes,
and an image comes to me of the workers
who made all this centuries ago—where did
they get the shells, the rocks, the plan, the stones?
I think of Italians I know from Queens
who still practice the craft of their ancestors—
do the descendants of this Shell-Master
have shops on the boardwalk in Wildwood
or maybe Ocean City, selling knick-knacks,
taking special pride in mini-Baroque
shell mansions, telling tales of fabulous
palaces built by ancestors on some island
they will never see, whispering *A Saint lived there.*

It's good to get outside in the Gardens.
We survey the terraced choreography,
the English Garden, the Garden of Love,
riotous rhododendron and azalea

alleys, with white peacocks wandering
everywhere as we rise to the Amphitheatre
with statues and pilgrim shells, crowned by rampant
Unicorn, the Borromeo family symbol,
reigning on the island's highest point.
Abandoning any attempt to assess
the landscape design, I think of all this rich
dirt brought here from somewhere—boatloads of it,
the finest soil. I smell it, run some through
my fingers—it would take several summers
of pickup truckloads, a million bags of Agway
topsoil and compost to start such a garden.

I hear a tourist say: "Mafia Unicorn."
I watch a woman—she looks like Sophia Loren
in *Two Women*—in garden clothes working
the dirt. Suddenly, the gardens are given
to me; I appoint her the head gardener;
we tear up flower beds and plant row on row
of garlic and leeks; vegetables of every
kind and color run riot among the peacocks;
we give almost everything away, we declare
a free pick-your-own-day for the citizens
of Fishermen's Island, where they have no gardens,
no dirt at all on that medieval rock.
It's time to go home—we get the last boat back.

FISHERMEN'S ISLAND: OFF STRESA JULY 2000

Up before the sun, walking the waking
island lanes, I stand on the lakeshore
and stare at far luminous hills where unknown
people lead secret lives of joy. Circling
the island I see many cats and women,
and three old men casting off in a fishing boat.
Where people still fish, most men rise early.
But it is mainly the women I see,
poised in ritual places the sun touches first,
gathering the sun, ripening, as if in some
fat mythical mountain vineyard.
Sudden fog rolls across the lake and burns
my throat like last night's grappa. Street cats gaze
at me, contemplating the Human Sphinx,
mesmerized by human multiplicity,
as I sing out loud and skip stones across
the lake. The cats do not regard me with
ironic eyes which see but have no vision,
which mock but never take possession.
How do they see me—am I inverted *Film Noir*?
And those mirror-jugs of water in doorways—
I thought they must be offerings to some Saint.
I asked the man at the store: "No, for the cats,
they see themselves, run, piss on some other door."

This island is a place to visit
in a dream, yet it exists everywhere

that it is, as quiet and real as the lake
is wet. The island is shaped like a fish.
By a strange lake you must empty yourself
for sleep (*Darl says My Island is a Fish*).
The lake, the mountains, talk to me. The lake
prefers intimate forms of address,
but the Alps refer to themselves in
the third person. In the rhetoric
of lethargy, I compose myself
for the next sentence. Wind moans over the lake,
wavetones break, howl like vowels, consonants crash
on rocks, leaking lake-language secrets.
I write in my head a noise that rhymes
with Nature, with brooding on God and Time.
The lines I write all wind and lean toward love.
I watch a young girl lead an old man gently
down to the lakeshore where he runs his hand
along an ancient fishing boat, rotting, half-sunk.

It is an island with an open heart.
I like the way the sun reaches into
alleys and crochets the green and red
fishing nets draped from staircases and porches;
I like the first sunlight spilled on the white
and yellow walls of red-roofed houses;
I like the way the spine of the fish,
the narrow main street, winds toward *San Vittore*,
the eleventh century church with the high
white steeple, and the fisherman's iconography
inside. I like the way the narrow side lanes
lead always to water, lake-and-mountain
views framed in stone; I like how it feels when
the first ferry comes and the last ferry leaves,
how the island returns to the Middle Ages.
Liking all this, the fishermen talk French to me.
All poets, all of us, long for a place
like this, a homeplace we have never known,
and we make in our songs the ghosts of the dead
we have never known, and we yearn to praise
a lost world that we never really had.

I do not seek the merely picturesque:
I walk the winding narrow street thinking
perhaps I will meet something quaint and old-
fashioned, like Marxism, like Surrealism.

We take the boat to *Isola Bella.*
Sparrow does not like the Borromeo Palace.
In the cool grottoes we feel like we are
in some strange shell-shop on the Jersey Shore.
We have a decent lunch by the ferry dock
before we return to *Pescatori.*
We keep reminding ourselves that we are here
in these islands to plan a conference,
to bring a crowd of people we love
halfway across the world to discuss
Hemingway. We are not here on the traveler's
usual mission of reverse archeology:
To use the past to salvage the ruins
of the present, place to redeem motion.

When Sparrow goes to the room for a nap
I go to the café over the lake,
built out over the water, and make notes:
Frederic Henry was here. Hemingway was here.
The Fisher King is mending his nets here.
I am here—the café is noisy and crowded,
tourists waiting for the next boat, I cannot
think. I write: *Hemingway Hermeneutics*
merged with Thalassic Therapeutics.
Perhaps something classically ludic?
Or a Deus Loci propaedeutic?
Writing this down after the first drink,
I realize I am not making conference notes,
I am writing deadly afternoon poetry,
indulging the cool clean martini-tickle
of fat farouche words, ridiculous rhymes.
(When I read it later, I am clueless.)
I know better than to scribble poems
after lunch in a café, so I put down
my pen and listen to conversations

at nearby tables. "Why must you always
be so *participial*," he says,
"always *becoming* something else. Just BE."
"Oh piddle. Participial." she shakes
her English hair, "I just want awe, at life,
and at the passing of life." "Every step
we take," he says, "leaves a trace we can't erase."
"Nonsense," she says, "the trace is not on place,
but how the place is traced in you when you leave."
Even the lake is faking, leaking poetry.
I wish the last boat would come and they would—

Leave. I shift my chair, watch a kid leaning
over the rail, looking at the fish, talking
Kentuckese: "Do fish get thirsty? Do they
dream of deserts? Do matches dream of fire?"
His father, ignoring him, proclaims to
a woman pierced all over with shiny things:
"When death comes around I'll be out of town."
I tune out, dial another table.
An old man, in broken English, seems to be
telling the story of his life, of wars,
exile, revolution, marriage and loss,
to his four young companions, who barely
listen, and chatter with each other
about the shopping in Stresa. The old man
talks on, but each chapter is interrupted
by one of the young shoppers who does not know
the price of things, the no-return no-refund policies.

The old man's voice trails off as if he knows
that when we tell the tale of our lives, no
one really listens, so we are reduced
to making a *Cliff Notes* condensed version
at best: who wants the whole text? Those who need
it most don't need it to pass the Mid-term.
(The Final, however, is another matter.)

The last ferry is arriving, bills are paid,
talk ceases, the café empties, I am

alone with my island. The waitress, relaxed
at last, sits at the next table and smiles at me
as if to say "Thank God the mainlanders
are gone!" At a distant dock, a fisherman sings.
The locals come back outside; the cats, too.
The lanes belong to the island again.
An old woman cries "*Santo Cielo*!"
at nothing in particular and the bar-
tender listens to soccer on his radio.
Sparrow walks down the lane by the waterside,
bringing the actual island with her:
"Isn't it lovely now," she says, "let's do
the conference, bring the people we love here,
give them this island." It is decided.

FISHERMEN'S ISLAND: JUNE 2002

For the Nick Adams Society

And now here we are again on *Pescatori*
and you have guessed the rest of the story—
(ah there I go martini-afternoon-rhyming)—
how we *walked* this island years ago, dreaming
you here; how I said *this is an island*
for walking; how I try to remember
now how it feels to walk—Funny, isn't it—
plan for two years to bring you here and then
you have to carry me? *Swing Low, Sweet Chariot*—
and how do you say wheelchair in Italian?
Oh these medieval radical cobblestones,
how they rattle my "enigmatic bones"
(as the orthopedists are pleased to call
my hips and knees . . . *coming for to carry*
me home) . . . Never mind. Through protocols
of memory, hierarchies of history,
we pass toward something that looks like Wisdom
but may just be Love at last willing to speak
the word. And maybe Count Greffi is right,
old men "do not grow wise. They grow careful."
Bones, he says, that break "like a stick of chalk."
(*Coming for to carry me home* . . . let me walk)

May you be strong at the broken places.

We pass, at last, from muscular Gnosis

to advanced avascular necrosis.
The divine afflatus
is diagnosed as crippling arthritis.
Sudden scoliosis meshes
with holy ghostliness of the flesh.
With old Ezra I say: "Damn Perhaps!"
                                                  And *skeletal collapse.*
                    How do we know the cancer from the dance?
MRIs, X-Rays, Bonescans, Complete Biop(oe)sy—
The Works: get it at your local bookstore.

Still, like a place-obsessed periegete,
or a fond father planning a family vacation,
or a wheelchaired patriarch shaping a family
reunion—ah! choose whatever image works—
what matters is this: making this island
for you has kept me going through the bad time;
hearing you all say "You must go—we'll *carry* you!"
has echoed for me (and for Sparrow too)
like alchemical love in dark nights of the soul—
a Voice crying: *Let the Wheelchair Roll!*

I really thought I might die here but what the hell
I wasn't going to tell anybody that. I didn't want
to be like the old friend who, for years, told everybody
she was dying: every conversation was about her death
I won't be here long and *This might be the last time*
I see you and *I won't be staying here long* (nobody
stays long) and then she stayed a long time and after
years she died and it was strange as if it had happened
long ago because she'd been saying it for so long.
As if she never *lived* the years she *talked* about her death.

So I thought what the hell and decided to put these words
in a sealed envelope inside my passport: *If I die on*
Fishermen's Island dump me in the lake pour some good
wine over me sing some songs and prayers consign my
soul to the Alps then sing and dance all night long while I
float far up the lake—at least you won't have to carry me.

However, now that I've eaten that feast at the Verbano—our Nick Adams Society Banquet with all the tearful toasts in the garden—I feel much better. Amazing what five fresh fish (*-er king*) courses from Maggiore will do for your bones: some Prosecco then *alborelle fritte trittico di pesci ravioli di pesce risotto al persico orata con capperi* some fried bleaks lake perch and gilthead seabream with local wine does it every time. I've thrown that envelope away unopened. We know that every quest, every pilgrimage, must be lived as if it is the last.

Now let there be songs and wine and tales of tall glory
Shantih   Shantih   We're Radically Free   *Isola Pescatori*

PESCATORI TANKA

booked two years ago
large apartment for poetry
readings and parties
with ten windows on the Alps
French door balconies on lake

hot winding hell-steps
in medieval building
fish-smell centuries old
fish-traps stacked along the steps
took five men to get me up

one to take wheelchair
up one to push from behind
one to guide my feet
one alongside to lift my
arm around shoulder and one

to catch in front: ten
minutes to climb or descend
those steps could only
do it once a day—*l'esprit*
of fishermen's *escalier*

when we reached the street
the steep narrow cobblestone
alley rough to roll
four men carried me in chair:

islanders watched crossed themselves

smiled and even clapped
once we were neighbors after
three days: sometimes when
all were gone to the mainland
I stayed sat in the sun played

guitar on the bal-
cony. Tourist ferry-swarms
took pictures of me:
"Oh look an old Italian
fisherman singing lake-songs."

Video cameras
aimed at me while I quick-plucked
strings like mandolin
sang high lonesome Bluegrass: fake
Italian words and phrases

We could stay here start
a tourist business our crew
said: charge photo-fees
pass the hat for songs at dock
I would mumble menu terms

like telling stories
Posse could translate for Brits
for a fee: we'd sell
some *hummel*-style figurines—
"Old Italian Fisherman"

I could sit and sing
maybe learn to speak local
we'd peddle *hummels*
whole new line of figures: first—
"Old Italian Fisher King"

ON HEARING OF THE DEATH OF TED WILLIAMS ON A FOREIGN ISLAND (OR, THE RITES OF THE FISHER KING ON FISHERMAN'S ISLAND)

For the Pescatori Posse

On the narrow cobblestone lane that divides
the tiny fish-shaped island, the spine
of *Isola Pescatori, Lago Maggiore,*
there is a small café with a large picture
of Ted Williams in his Red Sox uniform
on the wall.(DiMaggio you would expect
here on this Italian Fishermen's Island—but
Williams?) There, my friend, born long after the last
swing of that great bat, hears the news, comes with wine
and cheese and olives, to speak of tragedy
as we watch the sunset on *Maggiore.*

".406," I say, and I watch the room
to see who, among a dozen friends born since
1970, understands. Recognition flickers
in the eyes of the messenger, and one other
who relays the TV news that Williams' heirs
are fighting over whether he should be
cremated and his ashes scattered over
the Florida Keys he loved to fish, or
frozen for the future to serve who knows what

cryogenic fantasy—“Fire or ice,
aesthetics or science,” I say (and since

I’m feeling like I might not last through this trip
I add): “Are you guys gonna put me on
the refrigerator shelf between Ted Williams
and the cold beer? Or scatter my ashes
over my favorite Catskill trout streams
and, when you’re wise old fishermen, catch and release
me?” We talk some about Williams’ career,
about the old Musial-Williams debates,
in which, being a National League fan,
I usually defended Musial, reciting stats
and refusing to yield to all who praised

Williams as some kind of God in the Great Green
Garden of American Innocence.
I do it even now, though I no longer wholly believe
in Stan the Man; I do it because at least one
fervid Red Sox fan, who knows the legend
from long before he was born—the Splendid Splinter,
Teddy Ballgame, The Thumper, The Kid,
the god they loved to hate—evokes the myth,
recites the facts. A young neutral searches
the web, reports 15,433 entries for Musial,
only 14 for Williams, says Musial’s website

features Stan the Man playing “Take Me Out
To the Ballgame” on his harmonica
(good old Stan) and the Williams web is silent,
nothing but a picture on the frozen site.
I tell them about Updike’s take on Ted’s
legendary unresponsiveness: “God
doesn’t answer letters.” The whole time I’m
talking Musial-Williams trash with my thirtyish
friends who quickly grasp the mythic formulae,
I am thinking of my father, in 1953,
at Shibe Park, Red Sox against the A’s,

Williams’ first at bat there since he came back

from his *second* war; weeks before, I'd watched
Musial on the same field, against the Phillies,
and I was still imitating Musial's
famous corkscrew stance (even if coaches laughed);
I hear my voice intone the Musial stats,
and my father's gentle reply: "There's fact
and there's myth. There's .376 and there's .406.
Men who stay home and men who fight the wars.
But the main thing is—watch closely how he swings."
I watched, and I saw, and before the ball

left the park, I knew my father was right,
about wrists, vision, about who was the greatest
hitter the game would ever see. That brief
season, cut short by his service as Marine Corps
Pilot, Williams batted .407 in 91 at bats,
13 home runs, better than 14.2 HR%,
one every seventh time up, and I saw one of them,
and it is still soaring in Italy, in 2002,
as I talk with friends and students—beloved
sons and daughters—thinking of my father
(dead before they were born), watching my 70ish

elder brother-poet from Boston (who grew
up in Fenway dreams, hammering linedrive words
to envision the amazing fiction of Williams' bat)
fill up, weep openly, when he walks in, hears
the news: We are all one in the fire and ice
of that moment, in the arc of a swing,
in the dreamdark cast of the Fisher King,
an entire century bound together
in the vision of that provident swing
that breaks our hearts, even here, on this far
and peaceful Italian island.

Then they want to go to the small café
with the large picture to pay their last respects.
I send them off with my wheelchair blessings
and I am alone with my father, and history.
The wine open, I turn the corkscrew idly

in my hands, hear a voice saying: "Stand straight
and bat, kid. Why screw your body up like that?
You're twelve years old, almost six feet tall.
In a few years, you'll pass the Splendid Splinter."
And so I did, stood six-feet-six by sixteen.
I guess that's funny now, here in this wheelchair

where I sit exactly four-foot-six (.406)
and see the world a different way: like Ted,
six-foot-three, a Marine, eighteen years with the same
team, then all that fishing—they say when he fished
the Florida Keys, he outhit Hemingway.
This, too, is a Hemingway island,
a Frederic Henry-Fisher King island:
I wish they were all here now, and my father, too,
talking about Ted Williams; that's it though,
my father and Hemingway dead at sixty,
and Ted, the last time I saw him, in that wheelchair.

Ah pour the wine—*Semper Fi* ye Fisher Kings!
Beneath my window, I hear lake-waves wash
the silent island's rocky shore (*I would arise
and go now if I could)*—then I hear a stranger
sound, the whack of something I cannot name,
the crack of time from some ancient distant game.
I wheel my chair to the balcony, look down
along the lakeshore for the source of the sound:
There, in the dim golden light, a kid swings
a bat, hitting rocks high across the lake
toward the white monster wall of the Alps.

*

I watch him swing, listen, remember when,
in the 1950s, I came home from that ballgame,
stayed out late, in that vacant lot in the dim
streetlight from the cobblestone alley,
hitting rocks with my cracked taped Louisville Slugger,
long high flies over the center-field wall,

hot line drives rattling trashcans in the alley,
unscrewing my Musial-stance, feeling free
in my new swing and dance, twelve years old,
hitting every other stone off some distant fence
that echoed the report of my victory.

I hear my friends singing in the alley,
making their way home from the café—
"*Semper Fi* Fisher King" I shout to the kid
by the lake. He pauses in his swing,
looks up to the Alps, as if the mountains
have uttered his name and proclaimed his fame.

WHAT YOU DID NOT HEAR (AND FEEL) THE FIRST TIME

It can be useful,
as a kind of poetic damage control,
to revisit places you've written about,
to list all the things you left out
for reasons of craft, accident,
or imperfect attention.

Take *Isola dei Pescatori*, for example,
a place you wrote about at length,
trying as you wrote, to remember everything,
working from notes on napkins
and winestained memory.
Returning after two years,
staying in the exact same place,
it's clear you were not *listening*
the first time, everything was visual,
structural, and thus you missed these sounds:

> night cries of the island cats;
> scarce brave birdcalls at first light;
> sounds of trains across the lake
> and how at midnight you can tell
> the local from the Swiss express;
> how even the silence changes
> in the car-less island stillness;
> how from dusk to dawn you can hear
> the slightest shingly break of waves

on the lakeshore; and the hound across
the medieval alley snoring,
whimpering in his long-eared dreams,
and when you make a high-pitched howl
he answers back and the whole island
hears; and the sound of the trash-truck,

Pescatori's only car, at first light.
And there is something else you missed, not heard
but felt, through the soles of your feet and the frame
and wheels of your chair (walkers cannot feel this
you must be in a wheelchair): how on a hot July
afternoon, with ferries and pleasure boats
invading the isle, the very cobblestones
and slabs that anchor the island tremble,
a seismic rumble, toe-to-head passage
of deep magical *Maggiore* massage.
First or last time, walking or wheeling,
there's always something you'll miss feeling.

YEARS LATER: A MEDITATION ON MY POEM ON THE HOTEL WALL IN ITALY

For Silvia and DNS

Years later, my brother calls me from Italy,
from the Hotel Verbano on *Isola dei Pescatori*,
to tell me that he is on his way down to dinner
in the lakeside garden, to say that he has just seen,
matted, framed and given pride of place on the wall
of the hotel lobby, the *pescatori-poem* I scrawled,
presented as formal tribute to the hotel-keepers.
It is there, among the historical documents sleeping
off the terrible hangover of the 20th century.
Like another Verbano guest, Toscanini,
I seem to have entered history . . .
My bones feel rather post-historical these days,
strictly a struggle of memory against forgetting
how it once felt to walk tall in a hotel lobby and reserve
a table for dinner at lakeside, or stand at a bar,
or drive a car—all that feels more distant than old Ezra's cage
and Mussolini hanging by his heels, and all such rages
of the flesh. I make restaurant recommendations, local fish
from *Lago Maggiore*, and appoint my brother surrogate
walker, to take my place at the table by the lake.

Still on the phone, he tells me that Silvia,
the hotel receptionist, saw him reading my poem
framed on the wall; he told her he is my brother;

she is moved, says she has her own framed and signed
copy of the poem on the wall at her home;
as she says this, she places her hand over her heart.
One long distance tear rolls down my face as he tells me this:
I see her face, how she smiled as we passed
on the 8 AM Ferry gangplank as she came to work
and I rode my wheelchair to the mainland to talk Hemingway;
how she looked as she watched me hefted up curving stairs;
how she smiled when she brought dinner to our apartment;
how we wrote each other for a year before we met,
making sure that every detail would be right
for all the friends we were bringing to the island.
And as I think about her and how my brother
is on that island I can never get to again, reading
the poem I left behind, I realize tears are streaming freely—

and suddenly it's OK, everywhere, anywhere,
all the wheres we can never see and be
again, if we have given something, left something behind—

if we have worked to make that island real for two dozen friends,
have given it as a precious gift to tribal brothers, daughters and sons
who may someday return there and think of us, send a card,
read a poem on the wall, remember with a hand held over the heart
(and even for those who have already forgotten we *took* them there,
made that place for them and as they look at pictures of themselves
they think *they* found the place)—

and if that something is a poem read by a brother
on his way to dinner and if he is moved and she,
watching his face, remembers everything and puts her hand
(as if in some fine old sun-flooded painting) softly on her breast
(a gesture to break the hardest heart)—

So I weep for all the places we cannot go again, all
the places we have truly lived, loved and given,
and thus left behind, lost and regained deeper parts of ourselves
and in time's dark mystery let them write this obituary:
"He had a gift for giving places that he loved"

With my hand held over the heart of the world I sing for all
of us traveling, going, returning, reading and writing the walls
of the world's hotels: the voyager's mark of immortality—
a song left here, a poem there, an image inscribed in Italy,
an icon saluted with a hand on the soul of memory.
A swift and secret smile shared in the lakeside garden,
on the curving staircase, on the early morning ferry.

The poem referred to here, the one that now hangs on the wall of the Hotel Verbano (and in Silvia's home) is the first poem in this Borromean sequence.

3.

VARIATIONS

THE HEMINGWAY VARIATIONS: SPINNING THE CENTENNIAL (1999)

I
A man can be decanonized but not defeated.

II
"I'm not going to be one of these bitches
That ruins children," she said. "It makes
One feel rather good deciding not to teach
Great literature." *I said nothing.*
"It's sort of what we have instead of Hemingway,"
She said. *"Some people have Hemingway,"*
I said. "Quite a lot."

III
The new 1999 paperback, *The Sun Also Rises,*
Has this front-cover emblem: "The Hemingway Century."
OK, but the back-cover, quoting the *New York Times,*
Say's the novel's "tenderly absurd."
To read it, you must toss this paperback to the birds.
Get an old hardcover copy and keep it close.

IV
All 20th century American fiction comes
From one book by Ernest Hemingway
Called *The Sun Also Rises.* If you read it
You must not stop.

V

Road to hell paved with unbought stuffed novels.
Not my fault. Never been daunted. Let's not get
Daunted. We'll be daunted after three more Pernods.
Sun-Also-Rises like your you-know-what
If you have one.
One's an ass to leave Paris.
We circled the island. We stopped on the bridge.
He was still there, looking downriver.
We looked down the river with him
At Notre Dame.

VI

He was in his poem where he had made it.

VII

He wanted to paint country like Hemingway
Had written it. He felt holy about it.

VIII

It was a long time since he had looked
At the words in the water,
The way they held steady,
Tightened against the current.
They were very satisfactory.

IX

It is impossible to believe the emotional
And spiritual intensity and pure, classic beauty
That can be produced by a writer, a typewriter,
And a white sheet of paper. If you do not choose
To believe it possible and want to regard it all
As nonsense you will be able to prove you are right
By reading almost all writers who have ever written,
Including nearly every writer writing now, in whose work
Nothing magical occurs. But if you should ever
Read the real thing you would know it. It is an
Experience that either you will have in your life
Or you will never have.

X

They all think they *know* Hemingway
Except those who have *really* read him
And are reluctant to talk about the mystery.

XI

It was the shadow of the leaves
Of the tree that moved slightly in the wind.
It was that and a certain cleanness and order.
Some lived in it and never felt it.
It was our Papa who art in Nada . . .
Give us this Nada our daily Papa . . .
Hail Papa full of Nada—
O O O 000 O O O—
San Juan de la Cruz is with thee.

XII

Easter 1999: It's not the economy, stupid—it's the world.
When you fight, Papa said, you fight to win.
Boots on the ground or nothing. Yeah right. The Liberation
Of Paris, or Belgrade or Pristina—a picnic
With Apaches and ground troops. Montenegro's
Next. Then Bulgaria Albania Greece who knows?
My word yes a most pleasant picnic.
Funny how the very train the kid Hemingway rode
Through Serbia, maybe some of the same *wagons*,
Eight decades ago, to see the refugees,
The women with the dead babies,
Is the same train,
The Midnight Special of Ethnic Cleansing.

Before these train rides, in some lost valley
Village, huddled for a week in some basement
Waiting to be shot. Then the exodus, the raised
Arms in the hungry mob at the border, hands reaching
For stale bread. Camera close-up: *she lost her father*
Eight brothers and her baby this week but now
She looks happy in the snow with her loaf of bread.
This is My Body. Welcome to the Caliphates.

Welcome to the Crusades. Welcome to World War Three.
The women with their dead babies. All the nice chaps.
In another lost valley the Serbian nuns at the ancient
Convent and the Serbian farmers rooted there for 500
Years survey their poisoned fields and livestock:

Stiff-legged hogs rot and litter the lots behind
The single village street. An old man stands sentry
With a World War one vintage rifle. The KLA
Has struck again. This time they only kidnapped
Three Serbian children. "Why does the West,"
The old man asks, "give the KLA such deadly
Weapons?" The film-maker says nothing.
The old nun, weeding in the ancient convent garden,
Shakes a handful of weeds at the camera, asks:
"Why does the Christian West support Muslim expansion?"
You will not see this newsreel on our network TV.
All the paradoxes—I need a paradoxygen mask.
It's Easter morning and Belgrade is burning:

Over pre-Mass coffee I watch the flames explode
On the TV screen, see the train we rode three decades
Ago, our passports confiscated by the nice chaps,
Altercations at the border. Watch the bombs hit the streets
Where we once walked. Watch the Pope pray for the River
Of Refugees. I study the sealed Macedonian frontier,
The Albanian mothers holding tight to dying babies
In the freezing rain, waiting for the border to open.
It's NATO's 50th Anniversary. *Some Happy Anniversary.*
Sparrow is in the kitchen weeping, reading
Another Kosovar mother's book, reading Mother Teresa's
Diary. The single token Serb on CNN says that changing
Demographics threaten Sacred Serbian Sites.

Before the commercial, the announcer says:
"Easter is not until next week in Serbia"

This week I got so I dreamed about things—
It is all a most pleasant business
My word yes a most pleasant business

XIII

Summer 1961: I am working as what they call
The Social Director at what they call a Dude
Ranch in Northern Michigan, just down the road
From Hemingway's Petoskey and Horton Bay.
I am there for the songs, the girls, not Hemingway.

When I get my paycheck I go to the village bar
And drink with the lumberjacks and the fishermen.
It is the second of July. Firecrackers, Cherry
Bombs shatter the night, shudder and split the streets.
The village is preparing to celebrate the Fourth.

Inside on the big old green-tinted TV high over the bar
We hear the news, the shot heard round the world.
The shots that ring out the Lost Word,
The shots we remember better, where we were,
Who we were with, than those High Noon new frontier

Shots two years later in Dallas. Grave TV voice intones;
Hemingway dead from gunshot accident in Idaho.
But the bar community immediately decides—
This cannot be an *accident*, not Papa, must be suicide.
An old whitebearded man, like some ancient lost Nick

Adams, sits at the end of the bar, crying over beer,
Saying over and over again: "Papa betrayed us.
Papa betrayed us." I did not know what all
he meant, what Papa had meant for most of the century.
But even then, just a kid, I knew it was not betrayal.

Oh hold him tight he is in much pain
Hold him very tight
We owe God a death
But I am utterly unable to resign myself
Those of us who know walk very slowly

And we look at one another with infinite love
And compassion Twenty years later, Mary,

In double-martini tears told me how it was that morning
When she heard, when she found her husband.
And Renata was not there no one was there

To give the grace of a happy death
But Mary said they laughed,
Sang old folksongs on his last night.
The huge filthy birds are hunched hyenas
Whimpering bicycle policeman coming

And there, through that waterfall,
Toward that mountain, that House of God
Great, high, and unbelievably white in the sun—
Is that where we are going to sing
Happy Birthday Papa?—Happy Hallelujah Birthday anyway.

XIV

Let us cross over the river into the trees
And rest in the shadow of the next century.

FITZGERALD VARIATIONS: (OR, THE POET-TROUBADOUR, WITHOUT BENEFIT OF TEXT, TRIES TO RECALL WELL AFTER MIDNIGHT AND WINE HIS FAVORITE FITZGERALD LINES)

I

Reserving judgments is a matter of infinite hope.
If I had listened to my father, as Nick Carraway did,
I would have known sooner what that means
and lived a different life in my teens,
wouldn't have been such a rotten kid.

II

An extraordinary gift for hope
a romantic readiness
I guess you could also call it innocence
The core of the dream
Heading West
At heart, moralists
Seeking Blessedness

III

We drifted here and there unrestfully
wherever people made poetry and song
and were poor together.
We were athletes, too, but we knew

the dramatic turbulence of old games
was irrecoverable, except in song.

IV
We still stretch out our *arms toward the dark water*
in a curious way but we no longer mistake
the sea-rocks for docks
and in the unquiet darkness
the ocean-light is not green

V
Within and without
Simultaneously enchanted and repelled
In your twenties it's good to be compelled
By double vision

This sequence written for and first performed at The Fitzgerald Museum in Montgomery, Alabama: January 18, 2007.

But if you wish to live past 40
Precision and judgment are required
As long as the single window
Has the right view
And lets in enough light

VI
Other people are careful
They're the ones who get killed
When they believe in the green light
And suddenly meet those who run red

VII
One man could start to play
with the faith of fifty million people.
I suppose it happens every day
but we *must* still be staggered by the idea.

VIII
Clocks always *tilt dangerously*
at the pressure of the head—
past, present, future
Twilight Savings Time—
The past can never be repeated
And it never happened
If it was just an abstraction

IX
Sprang from his Platonic conception of himself
Service of a vast, vulgar and meretricious beauty
Overwhelming self-absorption ineffable gaudiness—
Faithful to the end to invented identity—
Maybe we all have some Gatsby in us, and it isn't pretty,
isn't all that great. As much as I hate to say it,
I suppose I was Gatsby. Really, I was Gatsby.
Scorned and rejected my parents very early.
Moved far away very young, forged a new identity,
a long way from home. Changed my name.
Knew bad characters, bad influences,
all those phony Codys. Read lousy books,
maybe even made lists. Worked for gangsters.
Knew lots of tackiness and sleaze,
immersed in the ineffable gaudiness of America.
But I never liked fake books, fake houses.
I was lucky to meet several Nick Carraways
when I was young. And I didn't fall in love with Daisy,
though I certainly knew her, many Daisys and Jordans,
and saw the dangers. Did I mention I never got rich,
though sometimes I lived like I was rich.
Now I live in a large four-storey house perched above
the Hudson River, which is not Long Island Sound—
and there's no green light on the Vanderbilt dock
across the river, although we have our share of fake
McMansions in the neighborhood. Old money and
family, too. But if I stretch out my arms across the river
these days it's toward the dark shoreline
of the Roosevelt place,

there in the silver shimmering moonlight.
These days I dream of a wheelchair drag-race
with old FDR. He was a good guy—part Gatsby, more Nick.
I guess I always believed in the American Dream.
still do, the best of it—especially when I'm living
in France or China. And I still know in my bones
what the first settlers felt when they held their breath
in the presence of this continent, even if my people came
long ago in the 1600s—maybe because of that.

Speaking of bones, the doctors tell me mine
are collapsing. Do not think I am making a self-absorbed link
between my current condition and the State of the Nation.

Yes, when I come back from Europe, especially by ship,
entering New York Harbor, or at Cumberland Gap
in Daniel Boone's footsteps, I still hold my breath
in the presence of this continent. All too soon after landfall,
however, you find yourself holding your nose—
So many things have a bad smell.

Actually, after thinking about this till 3 AM with 3 bottles
of wine I reckon that, unlike Gatsby, I did not spring from
my Platonic conception of *myself*,
but from my Platonic conception of *America*—
The land, the earth, the Garden, and the shining thing
in the mind that has always made me sing.
Maybe that's what saved me, if I'm saved.
Where's Nick when you need him to tell you
what it means and who you are and if you're worth
the whole damn bunch put together?

I guess Fitzgerald got it so right because
he was, in part, Gatsby *and* Nick.
And we get it right when we read
only if we see exactly how we
are Gatsby—and Nick.
That's the trick.

*

X

I just heard the news: *The Great Gatsby*
was the fourth most searched for book in 2006,
ahead of *Harry Potter* and *Catcher in the Rye*
and Madonna's coffee table *Sex*,
behind old Dan da Vinci's codes,
and *To Kill a Mockingbird*.
It must matter that AbeBooks.com,
representing 13,500 booksellers worldwide,
reports this news, and the fact that you can
get many used (*how have we used them?*) copies,
one dollar each, or a fine edition, a first,
(for a mere 45,000 bucks)
signed: "Affection to all, Scott Fitz."

XI

I don't know when I first read *Gatsby*—
Maybe it was in high school, that place
where millions of teachers and students
abuse great books, commit textual harassment
on the classics they don't understand.
I'm sure I read it before twelfth grade
where the teacher said it was like Hemingway's
Sun Also Rises, another pointless story about
a bunch of Jazz Age-Lost Generation drunks.
I know I hadn't read it in junior high
when my 8th-grade teacher Miss Evaul
quoted it in class. Miss Evaul was the only teacher
I had before college who knew and loved
literature and knew how that passion
could change your life. There was that whole week
when she made no assignments, asked no questions
in class, just told us all to shut up and listen.
She told us to "listen to the hum of the words,
the rhythm of the sentences"—she made us close
our eyes and *hear*. She read from Shakespeare,
Baudelaire, Eliot, Yeats, and Hemingway.
If anybody opened their eyes she'd throw an eraser
at them. She read from Dostoevsky and Ezra Pound.

A musician, I paid close attention to the sound
but I also looked through the cracks of my cupped
fingers on my brow at the girl in the next row,
her leg swinging up and down in the aisle.

Miss Evaul caught me looking and nailed me
with an eraser, right in the forehead,
the cloud of chalkdust settling on my face
and clothes. I shut my eyes and kept them closed
while she read from Fitzgerald. She said she was reading
the beginning and end of a very great novel
that we should all know by heart, like our favorite song.
I really listened—I took those words out of the class
with me, still hearing them when I went to the boy's room
before lunch and washed that eraser chalkdust
from my ghostly face. But I never erased
those words about *romantic readiness,*
about being *compelled into an aesthetic*
contemplation . . . neither understood nor desired,
face to face for the last time in history
with something commensurate to [my] capacity
for wonder and I kept hearing those words
even though it would be a long time before
I really knew what they meant and I have never
stopped hearing them. Miss Evaul kept me
after class the next day. She did not say she was sorry
about the eraser, said I deserved it.
Then she said: "You're not stupid like the rest
of them. You need to listen and keep on listening—someday
you'll need all those words." I listened. A great teacher,
Miss Evaul would probably be fired today.

XII
We were a sort of royalty, almost infallible,
with a sort of magic around us—
It's not just *Gatsby* we need; a little older,
everybody needs "Babylon Revisited."
Paris was my Babylon, too. The first
year I lived there it was like the world
of Charlie Wales. It was magic, the city

belonged to me. All that money, all that waste,
all those betrayals—long late nights unremembered.
Home at dawn. Friends who were heirs to famous
fortunes who ran up bar tabs in millions
of Francs. One of them skipped town,
disappeared, fate unknown to this day,
never paid his tab. Finally, we all pay.

*

XIII
believed in character wanted to jump back
a whole generation and trust in character
as the eternally valuable element—
Maybe we usually learn this too late.
Some of us learn it before everything's worn
out, before everything's gone.
Some never learn it. And they are the ones
who will make us pay and pay, forever.

XIV
And then there are the photographs—we all know
them: Scott and Zelda on the beach, all those
convertibles, tops always down, that pose
taken in their Paris apartment with little Scottie,
that dance routine in front of the Christmas tree.
You remember: all three have their right legs
extended like a desperately merry chorus line.
The ceiling-high tree behind them explodes
with gaudy ornament. Christmas 1925,
as I recall. I know I have that photo
in one of the 10,000 books on my shelves
but I cannot find it. But you know the picture.
As memory frames it, Scott's head is cocked,
Zelda's look is straight-on, intense, camera-locked,
her extended leg shows eloquent ankle.
And little Scottie's tentative legkick
is echoed in her worried uncertain look.
The Great Gatsby has just been published.

That picture always worried me, like a song
with cheerful words and undersong faintly heard
that tells you everything will soon go wrong.

XV
And then there are the journals and the letters.
Maybe you know that letter Hem wrote to Fitz
the same year as the Paris Christmas picture—
That famous letter where Hemingway sketches
his idea of heaven: a big bull ring, his own trout stream,
a fine church where he could be confessed
after he visited his mistress,
before he went home to his wife and children.
Then Hem tells Fitz: "wonderful country.
But you hate country. All right omit
Description of country." This always reminds

me that while I know Scott's vivid characters,
and always hear them speak their wonderful lines,
and I can dance and flirt with his women,
drink and talk trash with his men,
I cannot recall one intensely imaged
bit of country landscape in his fiction.
His landscapes are urban, social, with a city
distaste for the concrete particulars of earthy
terroir. There is no *place* in his places.
His characters are not, like Lawrence Durrell's,
a function of their landscapes. Whatever landscape

there is for Scott, it is mere extension, a function
of character or theme. In Hemingway,
you remember the country first. That's OK—
since we need both character and country.
This is not at all what I meant to say,
and you can feel free to steal this for your next essay
or conference paper on Hem and Fitz.
But in that famous letter, the real bit
that everybody forgets is that Ernest's
Idea-of-heavenly landscape ends with the image
of Scott riding toward Hemingway's Heaven

on horseback. The point is, of course,
they loved each other.
Hands down, the most compelling
literary friendship in American literature.
And Zelda was all wrong about it.
Those of us who have been lucky enough
to live long enough to redeem old friendships
will say: *If only they had both lived longer.*
They never had enough time to redeem the time.
I give them both, like an unbroken circle song,
like a golden apple in the sun of heaven, more time.

MOVEABLE *FITZ*: OR, WITH FITZGERALD AND HEMINGWAY IN MODERNIST HEAVEN

Maybe you know that old song that goes like this:
{Sung}—"*I dreamed I was there in Hillbilly Heaven*"—
and the singer goes on to tell his dream
of heaven and the great singers he meets.
Well I reckon I could make this a song:
{Sung*}*—"*I dreamed I was there in Modernist Heaven*"—
But since I'm just a recorder of fact
I'll set down with exactitude what I saw
and heard when I stopped by the other day
to visit in heaven with Fitz and Hemingway.
First we'll give syllable-count and anapest
and old fake pentameters the heave
and you can hum or singalong or feel free
to read this as prose (since most contemporary poetry
is prose all dressed up in typography)
whatever makes you happy:

In brief
  everything's fine
    in Modernist Heaven.
      All the old quarrels are patched up
        and everybody's laughing. I saw them all—
Ernest and Scott have resolved all the old
                                        tensions—
and Dos Passos and MacLeish, Sara and Gerald, Ezra and Tom:

allofthem,
  they're all very
    very happy. Even
      old Top Grumpy Aldington was cheerful.
        and Larry Durrell, free at last
from the need to seduce, mostly stood on his head
                    in the corner,
still wearing those same lecherous shorts with no underwear

First, I had lunch with Fitzgerald and Hemingway. I thought things might go south when Zelda joined us and brought up *A Moveable Feast.* But Scott and Ernest just laughed and then we were joined by a heavenly host and Saint Ignatius Loyola made some crack about Moveable *Fitz* and a blank as big as the Ritz. (Even Jake and Brett laughed at this—yes all the great characters were there too. But then maybe you didn't know that the really good created characters, like dogs and cats, go to heaven too). St. Thomas Aquinas and Count Mippopopolous joined us—gave Fitz a hard time about those late Count Philippe stories—you remember, the medieval stuff with the hero modeled on Hemingway the Lion-Hearted. Philippe didn't make it to heaven, but Hemingway did. All through lunch, Zelda flirted with me.

They're all good friends now. Always were, really. It was a very fine lunch with everybody very jolly even if Saint Augustine was a little long-winded in his explanation of the liturgical implications of Moveable Feasts. But when we heard Roland blow his famous horn and Charlemagne complained about the unceasing racket that sort of changed the subject and we all took a nap under the trees by the stream on a fresh green breast of moss beneath the medieval beech trees.

That night I went to the big annual event, the Divine Musical Comedy—kind of like a hometown dinner theater complete with audience involvement. Or a Variety Show, a kind of ethereal Felix Culpa Gong Show. In the opening skit Ernest played Fitzgerald's old Princeton role in *Fie Fie FiFi* –in full drag—and Scott recited his parody of Hemingway's *Snows of Kilimanjaro*, a spoof that showed how Hemingway was wrecked by his romantic awe of the rich. In the background the angels were dull and played too much backgammon. At the first intermission Scott and Ernest did a weight-loss commercial with illustrations of how many pounds of fat they'd burned off their souls drinking *gravityandgracemilkshakes* and eating *bigtwoheartedleanserenecuisine.*

In the second act, Zelda and Hadley sang and danced, a duet to some old Doris Day tune followed by some chaste half-nekkid kissing sister act out of Madonna and Britney Spears. Kerouac was on the front row with some old character he'd found on the road from Damascus, who sat there frowning in disapproval. His face twitched even more when Dos Passos did his Elvis Impersonations. Then Saint John of the Cross came on stage, dressed as the Dark Knight of the Soul, doing some old vaudeville routine with T. S. Eliot made up like Baudelaire. Old Tom really knew the Music Hall routines. The stage sets were by Cézanne. He kept right on painting through the whole show, as if none of us were there. His mountain kept getting bigger, until it seemed to hold everything, holding God very tight and steady.

In the final segment of the show, Zelda danced among the tables with a microphone, looking for audience participation. Johnny Cash read into her mike from the Book of Revelation. Hank sang a few lines of a song about a wooden angel. When Zelda got to my table I didn't know whether to sing "Amazing Grace" or "Folsom Prison" or read this poem. So I pulled Zelda on my lap and kissed her. Scott threw an ashtray at me—lousy shot, he missed. When he turned his back on us and went fishing in the lobster tank, Zelda said she admired my romantic readiness. But I figured I'd better cool off in the lobby where Dostoevsky was hanging out by the slot machines arguing and laughing about something with Pascal. Wagers, I'll bet.

When he wasn't selling drinks, Picasso sat at a lobby table selling bootleg CDs and DVDs, the latest batch just in from Hell. It's against the rules to mention those names. I guess that's to keep the lid on gossip about those who didn't make it. Wallace Stevens and Nick Carraway counted the proceeds from the event and bickered about the Idea of Order in West Heaven. Pedro Romero and Jordan Baker ran off to catch a gospel train. Tom and Daisy were not there, and nobody mentioned their names. Gatsby stood at the bar the whole evening, drinking green drinks, looking up, his arms stretched out toward something we could almost see. Picasso was also the bartender, kept putting too many big cubes in everything. Gertrude passed cookies, repeatedly. Gertrude passed cookies. She liked passing cookies. Liking her cookies, Ezra broadcast the whole thing on his

Divine Comedy Radio Show and announced in some endearing cornball voice his forthcoming five millionth *Canto* and his upcoming USO Tour with Bob Hope, something about cheering up the troops.

I loved them all and with love and laughter in the house it was everything and the way they loved me and nothing troubled my sleep. After the show, everybody ate fish except the King.

Like all Americans he wanted to go to Greece.

SONG AND LETTER TO BE DELIVERED TO BRUNNENBURG CASTLE

For Mary de Rachewiltz

I. "Song for Maria Down from the Mountains"

Down from the mountains all down to the sea,
ride rivers of ribbons and rosaries
into the shadows of the hidden nest.
Comes the pig-tailed golden-haired shepherdess:
gondola-leaning, canal-splashing tunes
sung to unholy waters of the lagoon.
Homesick for spring-water fonts of Tirol,
earth-daughter weaned slow from the soil.

Rocks and fields—the sheep, the cows, the horses,
the chanting of ancient songs and stories
when the peasants sit by the vaulted stoves
through winters longer than strong missals, old loves.
Homesickness, yes, but there was the Bible,
read in English, on his lap, and magic fables;
city walks, clacking of cooped-hen printing press
at Santo Stefano, where the ice cream was the best.
    Cantos in the evening.
    And always the leaving.
Oh let the villagers bring flowers and song, with torches and drums—
For all things in every place, all things human have their homecoming.
And we only know where we are when we are home

in the country of the heart and spring-glimmering stone.

II. "A Letter for Mary from Provence"

Who needs old fairy tales fat with magic
transformations, peasants and princesses?
I come to the castle with letter and song
for the countess who might have been the girl next door
in Jenkintown or Hailey, Idaho,
or at my farm in Kentucky on Boone's Trace
where, in another life, I was a peasant
clearing and working the land, fighting off redskins,
dreaming myself West. Then East into poetry.

In Provence, the Camargue, home of the other cowboys,
the idea started: an Imagist Reunion
at Brunnenburg, the daughters of Aldington and Pound
(who else could be found?) together in another century.
Catha and I sat in her tall hollyhock garden
in Les Saintes-Maries-de-la-Mer, talking castles.
Mary sent a poem for Catha. I made a book.
We wrote many letters, making plans.
Mary warned me about difficult access,
spiral staircase, stone courtyards and steps.
(These days I love nothing more than a wheelchair test.)
We wrote of gardens, flowers, weather, places.

Now Catha says her life has dropped down a black well.
She is unable to travel.
Each converging day, we understand better
how we are living and dying into each other
as we shape a paradise garden beyond weather.

An old country song goes: "Take a Message to Mary."
So I bring this message to your door, with a song,
a song of place and time with torches and drums:
  We who have been blessed to dwell in beautiful places
  know that "out of all this beauty" comes song for the ages

FOR EP: IN OUR TIME

I. Hôtel Pas-de-Calais: Paris 1972

They say you never forget the first time:
Paris '72—first time a travel agent
booked a room for me (and the last time).
I hadn't asked but she wanted to do
"something special"—it would be a "surprise."
We walked from the Metro to the *rue des Saint-Pères,*
checked in at the *Hôtel du Pas-de-Calais.*
Climbed the steps to the high room, saw her note:
"You are in the sacred space where Ezra Pound
revised *The Waste Land* in 1921. Write!"
We opened the wine and the windows
as the sky exploded, blossomed with fireworks.
The 14th of July, the Quatorzième—we forgot—
the Fête Nationale, my birthday. She had not.
She loved Ezra and had given me this place:
She hoped I would write here. She was a very nice
New York lady named Shapiro, with impeccable
gauchiste credentials for generations.
And *she loved Ezra* and wanted me to write,
to kneel into history in that place.

II. Campanolatry: Venice, 1972

A week or so later I was in Venice.
San Marco behind me, sat on stone rim,

contemplated pigeons, heard a strange hum,
turned to see an old man, wild hair and beard,
oldstyle clothes heavy for hot day, necktie
curiously knotted, fierce gaze fixed on
the Campanile. I thought he was some old
Venetian eccentric come out to croon
with the pigeons. Then I knew: *that's Ezra Pound*
I said to myself, and the stones shifted
beneath me, history leaned in on sunslant
wordlessness: I could think of nothing
to say. I waved to my wife walking back from
the *Florian* and when I looked again, he was gone.

I came back at the same hour the next day
(armed in *l'esprit de l'escalier*)
but he was not there. I stared at the Campanile,
hummed, wondered if bells had brought it down.
Later, I learned that he was there 14 July
(again I say, my birthday) 1902,
that morning the tower crumbled, killed one cat.
They had made it new, and there was a fine view.
But I thought of Philadelphia, how Ezra walked
the same streets where I was raised, professed
his faith at Calvary Presbyterian
where my great aunts sang in the choir and the bells
rang in the tower. I vowed to go to Wyncote
where I'd not been since ten. (I still must go.)
I thought how EP detested bells, he said,
the filthy racket of the London church-bells,
bloody campanolatry that cursed the silence.

That Fall, home from Europe, classes were dismissed
when he died—faculty poets (Christians,
Jews, and Pagans, left and right) gave memorial
reading, mostly from Canto LXXXI.
In the distance, village church-bells tolled.

III. Gregory at "the dulcimer" and St. Elizabeth's

In the mid-60s I ran a coffeehouse
called "the dulcimer," fashionable with folks
from Philly. A black artist known only
as "Gregory" hung out there, played checkers
and chess with all comers. Said he'd worked at
St. Elizabeth's, an attendant, seen EP
almost daily for several years. "A great teacher,"
he said, "lucid, generous, gentle but intense.
Made me want to be an artist." Even then,
I valued exactitude, so I checked out
his stories as best I could. They rang true.
(When he wasn't talking about Ezra,
he was sketching, painting portraits of my wife.)
With all the college kids who said the usual
things—it *was* the *60s*—he argued, defended, said:
"There was not a racist bone in Ezra Pound's body."
He talked about chess and checkers
with Ezra, about all the famous visitors,
said if St. Liz was a nuthouse then so was
Parnassus. Said he'd discussed Frobenius
with Ezra—(that meant nothing to me then;
I probably thought it was a Viennese
pastry). I took no notes, remember mainly
his open love for Ezra. I do not know
how old Gregory was, or his real name,
or what happened to him after I fled west
to Hawaii. I now summon him as witness.
His portraits of Sparrow still hang on my walls.

IV. My Father Explains Ezra Pound after a Hard Day at the Factory

My father was a newspaper poet, legendary jazz pianist,
factory worker. Crowned Poet Laureate of Atlantic City at 19.
Born in 1909, he said: "I should have gone to Paris—
but it was too late by 1930." Family lost everything in '29.
And besides, Paris was over then.
When I was a kid he marked up my fifth-grade poems.
(Later I didn't show them). But we talked about poets and poetry.
"Take Ezra Pound," he said, "An old Philly boy who went to Penn"

(Was that my first betrayal of my father—that I did not go to Penn
as he'd always hoped. Declined the scholarship. Didn't want to play
Ivy League ball.) He said: "Pound has a great ear, no not so much *ear*
as a great feel for rhythmic improvisation in tension with form."
(I didn't know what that meant until he showed me on the piano.)
He laughed about Pound's attempts to write actual music, opera,
troubadour verse-into-song. (I was writing my first songs then:
we co-wrote a few, he'd just close his eyes at the piano and say:
"Listen, hear *both* hands—doesn't this make it sound better.")
"No," he said, "it's not Pound's *music*, it's the stuff in his best lines,
the backbeat, the counter-rhythm, the riffs he plays like early great
jazz musicians, improvisation but no surrender of form, never free verse.
Like jazz before it went cerebral, became music in the head, no body."
Funny, how you remember certain things your father said
but you cannot remember the sound of his voice at the dinner table
asking you to *pass the bread, please.*

He recited lines as we walked down the street to prove his point
but because I had not read those lines in print I do not remember them.
(I was still reading Byron and Wordsworth). I remember only the way
the lines moved as we walked very fast, with a definite rhythm,
heading downtown. Just two miles. We walked everywhere, had no car.
We always walked fast because we had no money to ride the bus.
My father always hummed, too. We passed the Union Hall
where I played basketball. He said they were all Reds there.
When we got on the subway to cross the river he showed me
a picture in the paper of John Kasper who had been arrested for something.
Said he wasn't really Pound's friend, anybody's friend. Said Pound
wasn't crazy, any crazier than many other great poets. Said it wasn't right
for a great poet to be held in a cage or a nuthouse. Said if Pound's name
came up in school, I should watch how people talked about him—
"teachers doing a tango in a minefield," he said and mentioned
some eminent professor at Penn he'd heard lecture who feared Ezra,
and couldn't hear the sound of Pound's poetry. I thought as I looked
out the subway window across the Delaware to the skyline of Philly
and Billy Penn riding the city hall about how nobody in my family
ever talked about politics, or even how they voted. Everybody in my
family made music, played and sang all the time. That year he took
me to hear both Ike and Adlai Stevenson in their local campaign stops.
When we got off at the first subway station after the bridge, we walked

some more then he pointed to a beautiful brick wall, a tall house,
colonial stuff, said: "Who knows the politics of the man who *made* that?
Left-Right, Commy-Fascist, Stalin-Hitler, Mao-Mussolini—murderous
dreams *made* nothing that will outlast song. And that wall, that house
stands there and we can see it, enter it, two hundred years later
and be moved—by form, by beauty. Just like you can enter an old song,
the sweet shelter of a song."
Later, when my father died just before Ezra,
I looked at his collected poem notebooks, years of published newspaper
Poet's Corner columns, the necessary public rhymes and forms—
and in the unpublished notebooks, the cryptic lines, forms, scribblings,
unbearable music of suffering, song longing for beauty in the rhythms
of the factory; variations on "Pull down thy vanity"; his invented forms—
one that read down in the left *and* the right margins, perfectly aligned:
first and last letters of each line spelled: "What thou lovest well remains."
I remember when he got home from work every day in factory-filthy
clothes that smelled worst in July, my brother and I tried to be first
to say: "Paper please." Then he'd hand over the *Philadelphia Bulletin*
with lines of verse, song, drawings, strange multilingual words, formulas,
ideograms of history, written throughout the margins, in the white space
of ads, all over the whole newspaper except the sports pages.
All composed as he rode through his sixteen stations of the subway.
I studied his annotated newspaper while he played the piano
for an hour before dinner. It was my first glimpse of a world
something like the *Cantos*— (Maybe it was the Philadelphia water?)—
at least in that American voice, cool and cornpone,
an ear that heard and played Bach upside down,
elegant, perfect pitch, rhythm, formal and free.
At least in that enduring love of beauty

V. "Hailey, Idaho: Finding Lost Relations 1989"

Born: Second and Pine Street, Hailey, Idaho.
Forlorn mining town on dirt roads, board sidewalks.
They say you wanted to be buried there.

After the party in Hemingway's room
at the Sun Valley Lodge, then came the poetry
reading in our suite. Some Hemingways were there.

When the poetry was over, we heard on the radio,
much to our amazement, Captain Jack Stoneback,
Hailey Chief of Police, giving the crime report.
So we drove over to Hailey to find lost relatives.
Talked to Captain Jack about shared Pennsylvania
ancestors, from the 1600s on.
Then to Second and Pine, to the Homer Pound house,
Ezra's birthplace. Then around the corner to
St. Charles Borromeo Church, where the priest
told how Hemingway paid for the new church roof
and spoke to the Parish teenagers.
(We *know* why no biographer has noted this).
It's not the only time Hemingway made
a new church roof; it *is* his only talk to parish youth.

Consider the sequence: a few months before,
Ezra is released from St. Elizabeth's.
Hemingway sends him a check for $1500,
as he writes what becomes *A Moveable Feast*,
where he calls Ezra "a great poet
and a gentle and generous man . . . kinder
and more Christian about people than I was."
Says he's "a sort of saint," an irascible saint.
So Hem comes to Idaho, creates a new roof for the church
next door to Ezra's birthplace. Says to the kids
there who ask if it's hard to be a writer:
"All you need is a perfect ear, absolute pitch,
the devotion to your work that a priest of God
has for his." He says this, as if Ezra is listening,
still around the corner. He also tells the kids
to write every day but Sunday: "It's very bad luck
to work on a Sunday." Then Hemingway
buys a house just down the road from Hailey.

What is it about *paysage moralisé*
that professors refuse to understand?
Symbolic landscape's easy—*go there, see.*
The exactitude of this Composition of Place,
Hemingway's homage to Pound, is as precise
as Nick's camp, the Count's champagne on ice.

If only Ezra had been buried here,
they'd be even closer, with Hem just down the road.
Visit both graves in less than an hour.
We leave St. Charles *Borromeo*, swing around
the corner to Ezra's house on the way
to Hemingway's grave. I stop, pick some wildflower
I cannot name in Ezra's front yard.
The short drive feels like rowing all night from Stresa.
Captain Jack Stoneback, lost kinsman, is back
on the radio. I feel vaguely guilty of some crime.
In Ketchum I place the flower on Hemingway's stone.
In Hailey I found all the lost relations.

VI. "Venice/Brunnenburg 2007"

See, I return to the world's worst wheelchair
wonderland, the "disabled nightmare of Venice,"
to Calle Querini to chant litany,
to the stone castle on the mountaintop,
to Brunnenburg to cliff-climb spiral staircase
and offer bright-bone songs. (Was it something
in the Philadelphia water we drank as kids?
I remember the bad taste, the odor,
the water fountain at Wanamaker's.
Old Philly code: meet me under the eagle.
And then there was that fake Wyncote castle.
The Delaware smelled like the Grand Canal.)
O God of waters, *Purifiez nos eaux,*
Purifiez nos coeurs in the shadow-
poeia of the night litany, the beauty
of sinking cities, rising mountain-glory:
All that is loved well shall be sung, shall endure.

POUND CALLS ME COLLECT FROM PURGATORY, PARADISO, DOVUNQUE

Phone rings in the middle of the night: Caller ID
reads "Pound *Dovunque.*" Then that *voice* says:
Ez here. Pound calling from Purgatory.
I rub my eyes, look at the clock: Three AM.
Must be six hours later *chez purgatoire*
or maybe there is no Time in the mystic choir:

Look-here kiddo I been meaning to ask you wot
the bleeding hell this Hymnagistes thing is all about?
He says something I miss in pigeon-talk but I'm awake
now, try to explain Katrina, and how inspired by *Imagisme,*
we came up with this business called *Hymnagisme.*
"Started a few years ago in the Hudson Valley—

or in Aldington's garden in Saintes-Maries-de-la-Mer—
spread from there until now it's almost everywhere."
While I talk Ez hums in the background. Then he says:
The Faun was OK. Young Richard was all right. He still
around down there? "I meant *Catha's* garden, his daughter."
Ah now I see and does she know my daughter Mary sweet

Mary oh how I miss her. I explain that I've tried to get
them together with no luck yet. Then he brings up Hemingway:
Hem I miss Hem did I ever tell you I dreamed of Hem
at the exact moment he shot himself dreamed he was in the room

with me then Mary woke me up and told me the news
that was at Brunnenburg as if his soul dropped by the castle

on his way to the House of God Killamoonjaro you know
I'd been trying to get Hem to come to the castle since I got out
of that St.-Liz-loony-bin so at last he came but I ain't seen him
since guess he moved on from Purge-a-story before I got here
must have had damn good insurance what with suicide and all that
We talk about Hemingway. I tell him many *Hymnagistes*

come to Pound through Hem. *That boy could write like an angel*
always aware of the devil Ez says. *He sent me a check you know*
fat check lotsa dough when I got out of St. Liz. Did not cash it
preserved it in plexiglass. "I know. Mary showed it to me when
I was at Brunnenburg. You wrote on the back *this check is not*
negotiable permanently non-endorsable unfit for transfer

on a declining planet it may be endorsed to account of Mr.
Hemingway, Bank of Karma, Paradiso, Dovunque. When Mary put
it in my hand I think we both cried." *You've been to my daughter's*
castle then? "Yes." *Dear sweet tough loving Mary how I miss her*
next time you see her give her a hug hold her tight for me. "I will."
Then he rattles on about Purgatory for awhile naming lots of names:

There's even red Roosians here blackshirts too closet Christians
and anybody you can name Jews of course you know I never hated
Jews just got confused and anyway old Spire is here with me after
he lived almost forever and we have a fine time together
talking about poetry Then he tells me urgently in hoarse whisper
to warn young *Hymnagistes* about getting all screwed up

by politics and economic theory and *by all the Amy's.* Asks more
about *the mouvemong* I says it's not a movement not a school just
a will to sing informed by many things including something Allen
Tate told me about "illumination and praise"—he interrupts *that boy*
Allen had some dome some eye for women he and Hem got along
great at first— he was here when I first got here but he's moved

on up then he says something about Ginsberg stopping by soon
for tea he'll have to hang up *when first I heard what Ginsberg*

said about my deserving all the awards I reread his stuff
thought he ain't bad and then he asks: *Is this kid Dylan one*
of your Hymnagistes—"Not officially but yes"—*they sing some*
of his songs up here then he gives me his blessing his voice

trembling with intense hypnotic Nunc Dimittis—
says *this Hymnagistes thing you got going ain't bad*
so stay away from poli-tricks and d-con-omics
and try to write like Hemingway even if he couldn't sing
but I still miss ole Hem that's one reason I want to get
to heaven see ole Hem again. And the Possum. Maybe then

I'll be able to write some Hymns like he did and I always
meant to—"You did." *I did?* "Yes. *Purifiez nos coeurs.*
And *pull down thy vanity* moves more people than almost
any hymn." *Moves them where?* "To the place they need
to be. Maybe worship and humility. Clear-headed assessment
of courage order grace." *OK you've convinced me see about*

getting me in the hymnbooks I loved those old hymnbooks
in that church outside Philly—"Me too"—*and I hereby*
commission you to write the music choose whatever words
you want and I must tell you this: all my wrecks
and errors notwithstanding love is in the house
and I can almost make it cohere now. And one more

thing: see if you can get me re-interred move my
musty bones from Venice to Idaho you know where
close to that church where Hem bought
the new roof and talked to the parish Sunday School
kids about writing—Hope to see you but not too soon
remember I'm trying to be good so I can

get the hell out of here—that's a joke—I laugh.
From hell to Hailey and second innocence
And do this for me too: take a long long walk
through southern France, all through Provence
Get out of that wheelchair. "I'll try to walk it," I said,
"for you." How does he know that? Then the phone went dead.

"SHELL-SHOCKED: AN IMAGIST ON CASEY KEY"

For Catherine & Richard Aldington

Refugee from war-ravaged Europe, R.A.
moved to America, meant to settle
down, never return. Shell-shocked veteran
of Great War, WWII hermit on Casey Key:

found in Florida
his American Eden
patrolled lonesome beach

Gassed and shelled in that first war he hated,
in '41 reconned tides of Nokomis,
listed 50 shell species. Chastened Momus,
island retreat, nature's plenitude sated.

collected seashells
while Paris fell to Nazis
gathered butterflies

Still, always a patriot, though war-depressed,
served as Defense Deputy Sheriff
(Sarasota County), took the night shift,
the coastal watch for enemy agents:

they came from Cuba
the Antilles: saboteurs
caught on Casey Key

Daytime was a separate magic thing:
He loved golden dawns, mangrove roots oyster-keen
("a paradise where oysters grew on trees");
after storms, beaches like a Dali painting—

conch, coral, crabs strewn
sea cucumbers, sponges, kelp,
the Gulf's detritus

Mornings in his writing hut on the beach.
Noontime swims with his infant daughter—
(she gave me a picture—I published it later).
Writing her a children's story to teach

the magic of place
it's called "New Places are Fun"
(she gave me that too)

It's full of talking pigs and pelicans,
soldier crabs and mocking birds, animals
called Colonel-this and Major-that, cannibal
"two-legs" who make war-hell again and again

war is never far
away— the twolegged human
curse on Golden Isles

It's a sweet sad story the father tells:
the dignified black mammy, maid and cook,
her husband the gardener who also looks
after the girl, saves her from deadly snake, kills

it deftly with hoe
Aldington left out the serpent
in his Florida Garden—

his daughter told me a half-century later.
He would have stayed forever if he could
but money made him go to Hollywood,

where Imagists go to die: All idylls fade.

they never came back
to Florida, to Casey Key,
where they were happy

Biographical studies of Richard Aldington barely notice his residence in Florida, with scant detail, uncertainty regarding the length of his stay, and only a vague sense of where he lived. The author of this poem was the first to provide exact information regarding the place of Aldington's residence in Florida. I was able to do so (as this poem recounts) because Aldington's daughter, Catherine, gave me a copy of the short story her father had written for her—"New Places Are Fun"—which is set on Casey Key in the early years of World War II. Thus the details of this poem may be taken as precise biography available nowhere else except in a limited edition volume published in France that introduces and includes Aldington's Florida short story.

LUSTRATION? ATONEMENT?

For Richard Aldington on the 75th Anniversary of Death of a Hero

You demand atonement for your generation.
Purge the poison, wash away the "blood-guilt,"
"atone to the dead," appease the soldiers killed.
You walk the fine line between lustration

and atonement: lustrate, purify, banish
the evil regime. The oldest, saddest dream—
that we are innocent of the other's scheme,
that we can lift the curse, make evil vanish.

Each new generation must make its own
rites of atonement and expiation,
redemption and reconciliation.
War generations must urgently atone.

It may be folly to think we can redeem
the time, it is not for us to pardon.
I speak these words in your daughter's garden
in another century you have not seen,

after many wars you have not known:
You are not alone, I read, I am your child—
at-one-ment, all dead heroes reconciled.
Writing is all *we* can do to atone.

Written for Richard & Catherine Aldington and first read in Catha's garden, "Mas les Pellegrins," Les-Saintes-Maries-de-la-Mer, France 6 Juillet 2004.

THE RPW VARIATIONS

For Francesco Paolo Lovecchio (Frankie Laine) 1913-2007 & Robert Penn Warren (Roberto Pennolo Warrenecchio) 1905-1989: Requiescat in Pace

I

Autumnal Brother to the Old Wild Goose: Or, to V or not to V
(for the Neighborhood Goose)

When I was a kid and chanting along
with Frankie Laine were you singing it too—
Oh my heart knows what the wild goose knows—
deep in your *heart of autumn* your longing

for creaturely certainty for fathomed destiny
your *V upon V* (that adds up to *W*)
your *unwordable utterance* in goose-
talk: *let me fly let me fly let me fly away*

I remember Frankie Laine's song better
than I recall your old poem, more exactly—
my heart knows wild goose brother goose a heart
at rest—and did you say your heart was *impacted*?

Before I send some critic off on a wild
goose chase for your sources perhaps I should
reread your poem but I'd rather keep
singing hearing our voices sing together

wild goose cry hanging north in the lonely

sky tried to sleep it warn't no use you only
wanted to fly and know your own story
to feel tingling transformation of identity

in some imagined natural *V-formation* joy
some wordless flight that words would not betray
beyond self-conscious paralysis of irony
and so you stretched out your poet-arms to fly:

But isn't all this Osmosis of Being
just a sad case of Necrosis of Seeing?
I swear this: before I'll reread Whitman
I'll enlist as Uncle Ezra's hit-man

It all just seems too loosey-goosey—Look!
See that lone goose circling out of the *V*
refusing the pattern, sky-writing his
all-too-human-*?*—his uncertain question-mark

descending to live year-round in some small town
behind the convenience store, beyond the cars
parked by the bar where they hold Poetry
Readings, watching with scorn the overhead

keening flight of his kind, for him their *V*
not an emblem of achieved identity
or Victory, not even a disciplined
response to autumnal panic

just the tedious twitch of aerodynamics
surely not some well-crafted meta-mechanics:
I stretch my arms. I do not feel the tingle
but because I love you both I will sing—

hell why not?—with you and Frankie Laine
who wants me to go *where the wild goose goes*
brother goose heart at rest soaring on sweet small
southern breeze singing knowing what he knows

II
Variation: After Reading *Departure*

When was that summer when we sang what we heard in the streets
when all that we read—even the newspapers—we tried to believe?
When we stacked our suitcases, packed our bags, at a moment's

notice, thinking motion and distance would make a difference?
When we walked exotic beaches and studied extreme tides
like lessons of history—and felt insistent need to choose sides?

That was long ago, and now we only know that we go,
that we ride ancient choices, the body's whims, the heart's slow
mastery of love, the mind's reluctance to chant old hymns

of *Arrival, Departure, Flights Delayed* for destinations dim.
Yet the ticket is never lost or canceled and the train always leaves—
All aboard!—they wave goodbye wondering: *what did they really believe?*

III
Dark Google of the Soul: Late at Night, After Reading *Now and Then*

I went on-line to check something you'd said
and I don't remember what it was—instead
I was bemused by items on my home page:

Compelled to click "Summer Salad Recipes"
and "390 Things to Do Before you Die."
Before I got to 50 I saw I'd done them all.

That made me edgy so I went back to salad.
Too late too much wine for salad I hit "search":
Typed in "Life"—182,000,000 hits revealed

in 0.23 seconds. Then I typed "Death"—
only 76,000,000 items illuminate the screen
(in 0.18 seconds). I am comforted to know

in this random *dark google of the soul*
that there are twice as many hits for Life
my heart is touched with the certain knowledge

that I will live twice as long as I die
my soul sings amazing-google-grace
though I've forgotten what I tried to trace

in your work: This is just to say, Red,
that I did indeed eat some salad
at 3 AM that you were probably saving

for lunch forgive me it was so crisp so cold
and if the lines I typed afterwards
(I append them here) echo or steal your words

well there's nothing I can do about it
too much to do before I die and all ballads
are a matter of tradition and the individual salad:

A.
What was that story I was telling you?
One that happened oh so long ago
That I felt I was talking in my sleep

Trying to get you to understand
The shape of words and talk myself awake

B.
We always reach and touch things that affirm
our existence: like plants in our gardens,
like stones, walls, gates, like all the seasons gone
we stretch to touch, like summers that drip drip
like a leaky faucet when we try to sleep,
like autumns I've forgotten how to spell,
like winter and some new joy in April.

C.
The sudden storm crashes in the first false light.

The lights flicker, the screen flashes, the night
is so old I should turn this computer off
before power goes and I lose everything

When thunder trembles the walls
   And lightning scalds the air
End all arguments for belief
    Need no reasons for prayer

Beyond the terrible illusions of Time,
heart-rage to read runic beauty of this world,
to inscribe the calligraphy of Joy
on the faded palimpsest of flesh:
hieratic hieroglyphics of bones intone
the lost liturgy, the soul's ceremonies,
the last and most mysterious word for death.
The oldest song we ever sing is love.
The latest thing we really know is Love.

WARREN-WALKING: WEST WARDSBORO, VERMONT

For Brad McDuffie & Rosanna Warren

To deep Vermont we made the pilgrimage
to stand and sing at Robert Penn Warren's grave.

We had Rosanna's letter with directions.
But getting lost makes the best connections.

We stopped at the old country store in Wardsboro
for sandwiches, for old-fashioned cream soda.

We ate and drank in the September sun
not knowing yet we were lost, had the wrong one—

This was *not* the General Store of the West.
So we were lost as we began the quest.

Under the untended Apple Tree
we watched the dropped apples fill with bees

—like counting how many people could stuff
themselves into a telephone booth—

The bees kept drilling narrow apple-wells—
ten, twenty entered—I counted as churchbells

tolled. Then the front guidewheels of my wheelchair
busted on the rough uneven *terroir*.

I shouted in the stillness "Thanks a lot Red!
I come to visit you and this is what I get."

The rest of the day, wheels broken, had to walk.
Driving up the mountain on a dirt track,

knowing we were lost, stopped at tarpaper shack,
talked to hill woman with eyes like wary hawk,

asked where the Warrens lived, where they were buried.
Slow, deliberate, hawkeyed, unhurried,

she said nothing as we surveyed the clutter
of broken machines in her yard, detritus

*

of no discernible purpose, all those kids.
Then her face close to van window, I added:

"Robert Penn Warren." "Yes," she said, "I knew
the Warrens. Very fine people. I used

to clean for them. Very fine people." Stunned,
I thought how strange and wayward paths conjoined.

She said we were lost, we had the wrong dirt road.
we had to go back into West Wardsboro.

(*I remembered Red's trembly handwriting*
On those letters he wrote me, how he inscribed

his return address in his last years.) She told
us how to find the house. "It's the Willis Road,

the cemetery, we're really looking
for, to visit their graves." "Come from New York,"

she said. I knew she'd checked our license plate.
She said: "You must be family." "In a way,"

I said. "They were great writers and we've come
to pay our respects. To honor them."

Perhaps she was bemused by our enterprise.
"Oh?" she said. "Well..." and her weathered hawk gaze

held us as she told how to find the graves.
Again: "Warrens—fine people." We waved

goodbye as she watched us turn around.
Her directions were impeccable. We found

the house, drove by, all shut and silent.
Felt regret for summers when Red invited

me there to visit: I was always in France
or somehow too busy to seize the chance.

I reread Rosanna's handwritten letter
(*thinking how her hand was like her father's)*

*

as we drove and saw how we had erred
paid heed to her *watch the woods for dryads.*

It would get dark soon, so we quickly drove,
as instructed, to the dead-end of the road.

Parked. Wheelchair busted, I was ready to walk.
We looked around, saw no graves, saw only dark

paths into the woods: He followed one, I took
the other. We shouted: "See anything looks

like a graveyard?" Nothing. He ran down his path.

I walked hard and far amazed at how fast

I moved over rough terrain with my cane.
I froze, studied the earth, seeking any sign

that anybody had been there. No tracks
of any kind: I had gone so far back

in and I knew that if bones were buried
here then Warren was the last all those years

ago. Hollered: "See any graves yet, Brad?"
Long pause, then far voice in stillness came back

echoed over distant hills: "No graves, Stoney."
Stood still, listened, alert, felt in my bones

something near, no fear, thought of rattlesnakes—
I know well how to kill them with a stick.

It moved: only a jackrabbit then one more
and I wondered if I stood over a warren

of critters, some labyrinthine den,
but saw no holes so started moving again.

Careful not to stumble over something
like the truth and break a leg, I began to sing:

Who walks these hills in a long black veil
Who visits our graves when the night winds wail

Then listened for Warren walking. No sound
from the haunted hollow hallowed ground.

Just the maniacal silence of rocks,
the whispering miration of trees talking.

Leaning against a tree, I hear Joe Blotner telling
me how you walked near the end, pulled self up steps with railing.

The scaffold is high and eternity's near
With sudden certainty I've felt before hearing

ice-bound tree snow-crash in moon-glistened woods
at midnight I know I must go back to the road.

I try to remember your favorite song—
Old Leadlegs and Red-Leadbelly (offkey) singalong.

I look back down the way we came and right
there I see the last epiphanic sunlight

slanting on those stones on the far side
of a clearing in the woods. Then I yelled:

"I found it!" He was so far away
I barely heard his reply but he came

running out of the woods in a few minutes.
Then we stood silent by the stones. I leaned up

against Red's, catching my breath. Then we each
read one of his poems, felt his voice reach

us from beyond the grave. Said a silent prayer.
Then I said: "Thanks Red for breaking my wheelchair."

Only then it dawned on me that I'd just
walked a mile in the woods, by far the longest

walk I'd made in seven years. You could say:
The Miracle of Willis Road Cemetery.

You could call it Warren-Walking, Red-Rambling.
Or say that poetry was a gamble,

a secret bet that made me walk the line
and Red had covered my debt one more time.